Antitrust damages in EU law and policy

GCLC Annual Conference Series

College of Europe
Collège d'Europe

Brugge | Natolin

Global Competition Law Centre

5

Antitrust damages in EU law and policy

GCLC Annual Conference Series

Edited by
Jacques Derenne,
Eric Morgan de Rivery and Nicolas Petit

bruylant

Pour toute information sur nos fonds et nos nouveautés dans votre domaine de spécialisation, consultez nos sites web via www.larciergroup.com.

Éditions Bruylant
Rue des Minimes, 39 • B-1000 Bruxelles

Imprimé en Belgique

Dépôt légal
Bibliothèque nationale, Paris : novembre 2014
Bibliothèque royale de Belgique, Bruxelles : 2015/0023/047

ISSN 2294-5571
ISBN 978-2-8027-4847-2

TABLE OF CONTENTS

Pages

III
DETERMINING LIABILITY

IV
CONCLUSION

BY JACQUES BOURGEOIS

The editors would like to thank Jessica Walch, avocat, and Alice Xavier, student, for their contributions to compiling and harmonizing various chapters of this book.

FOREWORD

■

VICE-PRESIDENT JOAQUÍN ALMUNIA

EU Commissioner for competition

The Global Competition Law Centre's choice to devote its annual conference to Antitrust Damages in EU law and policy in November 2013 was appropriate and timely. After several policy initiatives and an extensive public consultation, the Commission had issued in June its proposal for a Directive on antitrust damages actions. Thanks to the work of authors and editors, the proceedings are now published in this volume. They cover important aspects of antitrust damages actions from different perspectives. Some contributions offer an insight into the state of play of private enforcement within and outside the EU and others cast light into certain legal and practical issues which are not covered by the Commission's initiative. This effort by the GCLC is an important contribution to the ongoing debate about the future of private enforcement.

I had the honour of speaking at the conference. Back then, the prospects for the adoption of the Commission's proposal by the European Parliament and the Council were uncertain. In my presentation I indicated two possible hurdles along the path for adoption: the procedural discussions and the little time remaining in the parliamentary term. Few believed at the time that an agreement would quickly be found across the institutions. A few months later, events have exceeded expectations. The negotiation of the proposal has been a success story for victims of antitrust infringements and a remarkable example of constructive relations among EU institutions.

The Council reached a general approach on the proposal in early December 2013 quickly followed by the European Parliament. At the end of January 2014, the Parliament's Economic and Monetary Affairs Committee adopted a text to start legislative negotiations. On this basis, in February the co-legislators sat together with the Commission to discuss the outstanding issues and work on a possible compromise text. An agreement was reached in just three meetings. The compromise text was then officially voted by the Parliament at first reading in April during its last plenary sitting before the elections. The vote saw a wide majority of Members in favour, spanning a broad range of political groups. At this writing, the text is being revised in all its linguistic versions, which is required before the Council can cast its final vote.

The pace and success of the negotiations can be ascribed in part to the determination of both the Lithuanian and Greek presidencies, and to the Members of the European Parliament involved in the discussion. Despite initial differences, we all shared the ultimate objective as well as the belief that it was time for the EU to deliver on its commitment to make compensation to victims of antitrust infringements a reality. The result is a balanced text, broadly in line with the policy choices suggested by the Commission. Both the Parliament and the Council were inspired by the ultimate goals pursued by the proposal. The first is to give victims of antitrust infringement effective right to compensation for the harm suffered. This right, with very few exceptions, so far has only existed on paper, because of those very obstacles the Directive will remove.

At the same time, private enforcement should be complementary to a strong public enforcement – to which the Commission and the national competition authorities are committed. Thus, the second objective of the initiative is to regulate the interplay between private and public enforcement of EU antitrust rules in such a way as to make them mutually beneficial. The Directive will ensure, for instance, that those infringers who cooperate with public authorities to help them detect infringements and bring them to an end will not be worse off towards damages claimants than those who do not cooperate.

Once the Directive is formally adopted, it will have to be transposed by Member States into their national laws. The Commission will monitor the concrete results it will bring when the new legal framework are effectively enacted. The rising awareness we have witnessed in the last few years, in parallel with the Commission's policy efforts, are encouraging signs in this sense. More injured parties have tried – though often unsuccessfully – to obtain damages for the harm they had suffered. The Commission has been a claimant for damages, and following its example some other public authorities (municipalities, and even Member States) announced their intention to bring actions for damages to recover the harm certain infringements caused to them – and ultimately to the taxpayer. The trend that has been set in motion is also testified by the increasing case-law of the Court of Justice upon questions referred by national courts. One of the most recent cases, *Kone*, concerns the possibility for victims to obtain compensation from infringers for the harm they suffered, even if they were not direct or indirect customers of those infringers.

The adoption of the Directive is a cornerstone for the future of EU competition law enforcement. While other pieces of antitrust legislation have brought innovations, this one adds something more fundamental to the way EU antitrust law works. It is true that the right to compensation already existed, but this initiative will inject new life into it. I am particularly proud of this achievement because it empowers citizens and businesses, who can now directly reap the full and concrete benefits of EU antitrust rules.

Brussels, July 2014

INTRODUCTION

Eric Morgan de Rivery* and Jacques Derenne**

1. The preparation process of the reform package on antitrust damages, while of shorter duration than the (in)famous directive on lawn mowers, nevertheless took about a decade to finalise.

2. That said, there were real and formidable hurdles to overcome in preparing the reform package, deriving in particular from (i) the absence of a US-style "litigation culture", (ii) a great variety of disparate procedural approaches amongst the jurisdictions of the Member States (e.g. rules on access to evidence); in itself, this made it very complicated to undertake any attempt at sufficient uniformity in order to establish an equivalent system in each jurisdiction across the EU and thus to avoid forum shopping, and (iii) the fact that "big money" is involved in private enforcement; quite naturally, this induces "big resistance" from those asked to open their coffers once again, given the increasingly heavy fines already paid to public authorities over the past few years.

3. To complicate things even further, once acknowledging that all consequences of antitrust violations should be compensated, this then means that consideration must be given to the consequences flowing all the way down to the retail/SME level and, in some cases, to the consumer level as well (e.g. in the case of price fixing). Such process involves "collective redress", "class actions", and all associated collective litigation concepts. As these are mostly known through American TV series or movies, they may scare even the bravest of businessmen.

4. Notwithstanding this complicated background, things have evolved for the best. First, the visionary principles laid down by the EU judicature in landmark cases such as *Courage*, *Manfredi* and *Pfleiderer*, all insisted on

* E. Morgan de Rivery, Partner, Jones Day, Paris & Brussels.
** J. Derenne, Partner, Hogan Lovells, Brussels; University of Liège.

the role of private enforcement as part and parcel of any sound antitrust policy. Second, the European Commission and its staff demonstrated an indomitable energy, ensuring the issuance of an appropriate package in June 2013.

5. This package represented a great leap forward, as completed with (i) a proposed directive accompanied by several very useful non-binding documents addressing the complex question of quantifying damages, and (ii) several non-binding documents of the same date on collective redress.

6. The package introduced concrete solutions, in particular, to the following issues:

- clear probative value of NCA decisions;
- presumption (rebuttable, but a presumption nevertheless) of the existence of harm linked to a cartel;
- quantification of damages; and
- joint and several liability of all cartel participants.

7. Of course, the package did not fully resolve a few remaining issues to the satisfaction of all stakeholders, for example:

- how indirect purchasers can prove that they suffered from price increases passed down the chain;
- how leniency can be encouraged by protecting evidence submitted by whistleblowers, or how voluntary settlements may be promoted by, again, protecting the evidence brought by these companies;
- the possibility to make damage claims subject to interest; and
- the appropriate statute of limitations for filing a claim, etc.

8. This seminar sought to give all participants a clear vision of achievements already made in reforming the antitrust damages regime. The seminar also sought to provide an opportunity to imagine, propose and defend concrete solutions that may help the European institutions and national governments to rapidly agree on solutions on remaining issues, in view of completing the private enforcement adventure.

9. The seminar addressed outstanding legal issues, following a two-tiered structure:

- firstly, we clarified the current state of play as the basis for discussing specific issues; damages actions are hardly new in the competition field, and much has been said, decided, and adjudicated on this issue, both at national and EU level;

   - with this in mind, we asked PhD researchers and professors from universities across Europe (Netherlands, UK, France, Belgium) to set the scene for each session by presenting one of their research papers;
- secondly, we asked national and EU judges, government officials, various business stakeholders (in particular businesses and consumers), academics and private practitioners (lawyers and economists) to comment on specific points of the reform package (however, all MEPs contacted declined to comment).

10. Vice-President Almunia naturally opened the conference by providing insights into the Commission's policy and objectives.

11. We then followed the logical sequence of a claim for damages, from establishing applicable legal principles (Session 1), to initiating the claim (Session 2), and determining liability (Session 3):

- Session 1 (chaired by Jacques Bourgeois) provided an overview of the past, the present, and the future:
   - This included an exposé relating to the state of play of damages actions in antitrust law, both from the perspective of EU law (EU case law and legislation) and national law (national case law and legislation); national judges then discussed their own experience and particular issues.
   - DG COMP (with Eddy de Smijter, the craftsman of the reform, and his team) presented the proposal for a directive as well as the reform package, as then debated by both industry and consumer representatives.
- Session 2 (chaired by Bernard van de Walle de Ghelcke) examined the issues concerning the initiation of a claim for damages, and specifically: incentive mechanisms, admissibility (limitation periods, standing, passing-on defence), and jurisdictional issues.
- Session 3 (chaired by Carles Esteva Mosso, Director of Policy and Strategy at DG COMP) focused on the issues concerning the determination of liability, specifically: evidence, access to documents, interaction between authorities and national courts, quantification, and imputability.

12. Turning to the Commission's policy, we are familiar with its steady encouragement of redress (it suffices to refer to the "footnote syndrome": each press release for a cartel decision invites victims to sue the cartelists for damages).

KEYNOTE SPEECH

VICE-PRESIDENT JOAQUÍN ALMUNIA

EU Commissioner for competition[1]

13. It is a pleasure to be back to the College of Europe's Global Competition Law Centre and I thank Massimo Merola for his invitation.

14. Last time we met, two years ago, we discussed the public policy implications of competition control and State aid.

15. Today our topic will be the legislative initiative the Commission has taken to make it easier for the victims of competition law infringements to seek compensation for the harm they suffered.

16. As you know, last June the College adopted a proposal for a Directive on antitrust damages actions. This proposal represents a novelty in two ways.

17. It is the first time that the Commission submits draft EU legislation in the field of antitrust damages actions.

18. And it is also the first time that draft legislation in the competition domain reaches the Parliament as co-legislator under the ordinary legislative procedure.

19. The initiative can thus be regarded as setting a precedent for the way the Parliament deals with important matters in this area.

20. Why is it important to introduce a new EU law for antitrust damages actions? There are two main reasons:

- first, we need to ensure that all European citizens and businesses have effective access to compensation, and
- second, we need to preserve the overall effectiveness of the EU-wide system of public authorities that enforce competition law.

---

1 J. ALMUNIA, *Antitrust damages in EU law and policy*, SPEECH/13/887, European Commission, 7 November 2013.

21. As to the first point, let me add that the EU right to compensation is well-established in point of law, but the reality on the ground tells a different story.

22. Only 25% of Commission's decisions finding a cartel or other antitrust infringement over the period 2008-2012 were followed by damages actions.

23. To make matters worse, those actions were mainly concentrated in three Member States – the UK, Germany and the Netherlands – and nearly all of them have been brought by large companies.

24. Clearly, access to compensation is insufficient and unevenly spread in Europe. Often the rules are so complex and uncertain that starting a damages action in court means embarking in an endless procedural battle.

25. Insufficient, uneven and costly access to compensation is simply unacceptable in the Single Market; particularly in times of crisis, where the costs of an infringement should be borne by the infringers, not by the victims.

26. So, the proposal we approved last June aims to overcome the legal and practical hurdles that still exist in the vast majority of EU countries.

27. As to the second reason I have given you, the proposal is designed to optimise the interaction between the public enforcement carried out by Europe's competition authorities and the private enforcement that is taking place in the courtrooms.

28. Let me stress this point. Sanctioning EU competition law infringements is and should remain the exclusive task of competition authorities.

29. This is true especially in our fight against cartels. Cartels are secret clubs. There would be little hope of busting them without good leniency programmes to reward the club members that decide to come clean.

30. It is for this reason that the proposal gives leniency applicants legal certainty as to the impact that their cooperation will have on subsequent actions in court – and this is all the more important in view of the likely increase in litigation.

31. I will give you more details on the proposed Directive in a short while, but before I do let me remind you that on the same day the Commission adopted it, it also adopted a Communication on the quantification of antitrust harm and a Recommendation on collective redress.

32. I will not elaborate further on either of these today.

33. Let me just say that the Communication will bring clarity into one of the most complex and costly parts of a damages action.

34. As to the Recommendation, let me note that it is the first ever EU-level agreement setting out principles on collective lawsuits and that it applies to antitrust damages as well as to other domains, such as consumer or environment protection.

The picture across Europe so far and main problems

Ladies and Gentlemen:

35. Two words describe the damages-actions landscape in Europe today: ineffective and uneven. Let me explain why I picked these terms in detail.

36. 'Ineffective' means that many victims of antitrust infringements cannot obtain the compensation they are entitled to in principle.

37. One important reason for this state of affairs is that victims do not have access to essential evidence, which is usually in the hands of the companies that have broken the law.

38. To get hold of the evidence, most national laws require a detailed description of individual documents, such as "an email message from A to B, on date X concerning subject Y". It goes without saying that most victims simply cannot meet this standard.

39. Another obstacle is the disconnect between the rules on damages actions and the investigations carried out by competition authorities.

40. For example, after a competition authority finds an infringement – when it definitely establishes it – many people who want to bring an action for damages are told that they are late or have to prove the infringement all over again.

41. You will agree with me that this doesn't make much sense, does it.

42. Finally, the current damages-actions landscape is potentially problematic for public enforcement too.

43. At present, national courts determine whether leniency documents can be disclosed in actions for damages on a case-by-case basis – and on the basis of the national law.

44. And their disclosure orders may include the self-incriminating statements made by the applicants; a prospect that turns companies away from leniency programmes.

45. I hope it is clear to everybody that such negative effect must be avoided at all costs. As I said, leniency programmes are simply vital to uncover and punish cartels in the first place.

46. This much for the word 'ineffective'. I will now turn to the second term that I used to describe the Europe's damages-actions landscape: 'uneven'.

47. Today, applicable national rules are hugely divergent across the EU.

48. Take for example the value of NCA decisions before civil courts, which ranges from a straightforward binding effect in some countries to representing just a view on the facts and the law in others.

49. Or take the limitation periods for bringing an action, which range from one to ten years. And only a few Member States have special provisions for actions that follow investigations by competition authorities.

50. Finally, whereas many Member States require a precise description of each individual document for disclosure – as we have just seen – some allow the disclosure of whole classes of documents even before the actual trial starts.

51. Not surprisingly, this uneven landscape encourages the victims of competition law infringements to shop around Europe for the forum that gives them the best conditions.

52. This would be bad enough, because the Single Market must be a level playing field also in terms of enforcing EU rights. But it gets worse, because our practice shows that forum shopping is a privilege for the happy few.

53. Most citizens and small companies don't have the means to shop around for the best forum and – if they happen to be located in the wrong place – they simply lose out.

54. Let me tell you that I find this unacceptable.

55. Everyone living in the EU and every company operating in the EU should have the same rights and obligations when it comes to compliance with EU competition law – not only on paper, but also in practice.

Proposed changes

56. The Commission's proposal – once it becomes EU law – will make antitrust damages more even and effective across Europe.

57. It will make sure that all victims can use the findings of competition authorities in the courtrooms and that the decisions taken by the NCAs are proof that the infringement actually took place.

58. Also, all victims will be able to wait for the competition authorities to issue their decisions without worrying about time limits.

59. Thirdly, it will be easier to access the required evidence.

60. I want to be clear on this last point.

61. This is not about uncontrolled access to evidence – not at all. On the contrary, the judge will have full powers of control to avoid excesses and protect business secrets and other confidential information.

62. In this way, everyone has a fair chance of obtaining compensation; including the victims of secret and technically complicated infringements and those who have no way to know what evidence is available.

63. Finally, the draft Directive strikes the right balance between making the right to compensation real and preserving the exclusive powers of competition authorities to punish and deter anti-competitive practices.

64. I have already stressed that the text now being discussed at the European Parliament and in the Council preserves the attractiveness of our leniency programmes and settlement procedures.

65. It does so in the first place by giving legal certainty. A company that intends to cooperate with a competition authority will know which of the documents it submits in its application can never be disclosed as evidence in a damages action.

66. In addition, the text also sets precise limits to the liability of the companies that receive immunity. I believe that this will further incentivise leniency programmes and facilitate cartel detection, without which victims of cartels would never obtain compensation.

67. These provisions go to the core of one of the main goals of the proposal; that is, striking the right balance between public and private enforcement.

68. Let me share my views with you on this crucial point.

69. I am convinced there can be no trade-off between public and private enforcement of competition law.

70. In fact, the two modes are complementary: the former is about deterrence and sanctions; the latter is about compensation.

71. A situation in which an infringer is sanctioned by a competition authority and then compensates its victims for the harm they suffered should be the standard, not the exception.

72. Consequently, I do not see why a competition authority should reduce a fine to a company just because the same company may 'voluntarily' have paid damages to some victims of its infringement.

73. The focus on compensation and the central role of public enforcement show the truly European approach of the proposal; which is probably why it has been received rather well since it became public.

74. Of course, there's always room for improvement and I am happy to see that the debate on its provisions continues among institutional and other stakeholders.

75. In particular, I am happy to note that the debate is steering away from the usual stereotypes.

76. For instance, it seems that everyone now agrees that competition law infringements can harm any economic agent without distinction, be they consumers, SMEs or large companies.

77. As a consequence, there is finally a consensus on the fact that the proposal gives a better legal protection to any type of victim, while preserving effective public enforcement.

The road ahead

78. So, when should we expect to see the Directive added to the body of EU law?

79. The draft is now going through the EU legislative procedure, which involves the Council and the European Parliament. I am happy to report that good progress is being made in Council under the Lithuanian Presidency.

80. As to the Parliament, let me recall that it has repeatedly asked to be fully involved by means of the ordinary legislative procedure.

81. I did not spare any efforts to achieve this objective. Indeed, this was one of the pledges I took during my confirmation hearings back in January 2010 and I have kept it.

82. The European Parliament has closely followed the issue as it developed over the years and many of its members have acquired a good knowledge of it.

83. As things stand now, I have the impression that most political groups would be willing to advance quickly towards adoption – which is not surprising, since the text submitted by the Commission stays close to the requests the Parliament itself advanced in its resolutions.

84. However, the debate seems to be stalled in procedural disputes which may artificially delay adoption beyond the term of this Parliament.

85. Now, this would be unfortunate. I do not believe that this is what the victims of illegal antitrust practices expect of their elected MEPs.

86. Waiting for the next Parliament before the Directive is passed could also create unnecessary problems for the leniency programmes of competition authorities. A continued uncertainty on this point could seriously affect the effectiveness of our fight against cartels.

87. I am sure that this Parliament does not want to be held responsible for the implications that artificial and ill-motivated delays may have on competition control and on its own role as co-legislator in competition policy making.

Ladies and Gentlemen:

88. The proposal for a Directive on antitrust damages actions is a milestone in the evolution of competition law enforcement in the EU.

89. In 2004, antitrust enforcement was modernised. It went from the sole responsibility of the Commission to a responsibility shared by the Commission and the national competition authorities in the Member States.

90. We now know through our practice that the reform has strengthened public enforcement. I am confident that ten years later – in 2014 – we will take another big step forward.

91. Public enforcement will remain key – there is no doubt about it – but citizens and businesses will finally have a law to translate their individual rights into reality.

92. When all is said and done, the draft Directive is about empowering them. This will promote a culture of respect around the principles of competition and will establish a higher and more level legal ground in the EU.

Thank you.

I

STATE OF PLAY OF ANTITRUST DAMAGES IN THE EU AND OVERVIEW OF THE PROPOSED REFORM

PART I: ANTITRUST DAMAGES AT MEMBER STATES LEVEL

Barry Rodger*

93. This article outlines a key aspect of a recent AHRC-funded project on comparative private enforcement and collective redress in the EU.[1] This article focuses on the state of play of antitrust damages in the Member States of the EU,[2] assessing the use of damages actions as part of the panoply of remedies available to enforce EU competition law rights in the national courts. EU competition law has traditionally been enforced virtually exclusively by the European Commission.[3] The historical primacy of administrative enforcement in Europe contrasts with US competition law ('antitrust law') where private enforcement plays a significant role.[4] The US system emphasises the importance of consumer rights, and the greater possibility of substantial damages awards also enhances the potential deterrent impact of the antitrust laws. The EU Commission and various Member States have recognised that private enforcement should be encouraged and facilitated and there have been various on-going policy initiatives in this area. In this context there have been some attempts to ascertain the development of competition case-law across certain Member

* Professor B. J. Rodger, The Law School, University of Strathclyde, barry.j.rodger@strath.ac.uk. This article is based on a presentation by the author at the Global competition Law Centre, 9th Annual Conference of the GCLC – Antitrust Damages in EU Law and Policy, 2013.

1 See www.clcpecreu.co.uk. For a full account of the project and outcomes, see B. Rodger (ed), *Comparative Private Enforcement and Collective Redress Across the EU* (Kluwer Law Publishing, 2014).

2 Excluding Croatia and Latvia, which joined the EU after the project commenced, and was finalised, respectively.

3 Historically, the position has been broadly similar under Member State domestic competition laws.

4 See for instance A. E. Foer and J. W. Cuneo (eds) *The International Handbook on Private Enforcement of Competition Law*, (2010, Edward Elgar in association with the American Antitrust Institute); C. A. Jones, *Private Enforcement of Competition Law in the EU, UK and USA*, (1999, OUP, Oxford); R. H. Lande and J. P. Davis 'Benefits from private Antitrust enforcement: An Analysis of Forty Cases' (2008) 42 University of San Francisco Law Review 879.

States in Europe.[5] However, the aim of the empirical research undertaken in this project was to seek to comprehensively identify all competition law cases before the domestic courts of the EU where parties were seeking to exercise rights conferred on them either by EU law (Articles 101 and 102 TFEU) or the domestic competition law equivalents. The Commission's focus in this area, since the Ashurst Report, has been on damages actions,[6] yet it is clear that EU and domestic competition law are relied upon by parties in both sword and shield situations, including nullity actions, and therefore it is important to seek an understanding of how competition law rights are exercised in all contexts including damages actions.[7] The project was firmly posited in the debate on private enforcement's potential contribution to achieving compensation,[8] in a wider sense than simply concentrating on damages actions by considering the extent to which the rights provided by competition law are protected and accorded effectiveness in relation to whatever remedy is sought.[9]

94. This article will briefly outline the research methodology before reviewing the general research outcomes in relation to case-law data aggregated for the EU and in relation to specific Member States. It will then focus on the central issue in the article, namely the remedies sought in competition law cases across the EU within the project timescale to

---

5 See for instance in relation to Germany, Peyer, S. 'Private Antitrust Litigation in Germany from 2005 to 2007: Empirical Evidence', 8 (2012) Journal of Competition Law and Economics 331–359. In relation to the UK see Robertson, A 'Litigating under the Competition Act 1998: The early Case-law' [2002] Comp. L. J. 4(1) pp. 335-344 and 'Litigating under the Competition Act 1998: recent Case-law: Part 2' [2004] Comp. L. J. 3(2) pp. 85-100. Rodger, B. 'Competition Law Litigation in the UK Courts: a study of all cases 2005-2008' – Parts I and II [2009] 2 Global Competition Litigation Review 93-114 and 136-147; See also Maton, A. Poopalasingam, V. Kuijper, M and Amgerbauer, T 'The Effectiveness of National fora in Europe for the Practice of Antitrust Litigation' (2011) 2 (5) Journal of European Competition Law and Practice 489-508 – focusing on the law in Germaany, Netherlands and UK and also Maton, A. Latham, S. Kuijper, M and Amgerbauer, T 'Update on the Effectiveness of National fora in Europe for the Practice of Antitrust Litigation' (2012) 3(6) Journal of European Competition Law and Practice 586-596; see also B. Rodger, *Article 234 and Competition Law: An Analysis* (The Hague, Kluwer Law International, 2008)

6 See V. Milutonivic, *Right to Damages' Under EU Competition Law* (2010 Kluwer Law International).

7 A. P. Komninos 'Private enforcement in the EU with emphasis on damages actions' ch 4 in *Handbook on European Competition Law* (vol 2) I Lianos and D Geradin (eds) (2012, Edward Elgar).

8 R. H. Lande and J. P. Davis 'Benefits from private Antitrust enforcement: An Analysis of Forty Cases' (2008) 42 University of San Francisco Law Review 879 (see also R H Lande 'benefits of Private Enforcement: Empirical Background' in Foer and Cuneo supra pp. 3-11).

9 See W. Wils, *Principles of European Antitrust Enforcement* (2008, Hart Publishing) at pp. 50-51 where he assesses 3 goals of private enforcement – clarifying and developing the law; deterrence and compensation.

assess the role of damages actions within the broader context of the private enforcement of EU and national competition rules. The article will end with brief conclusions based on the research outcomes.

SECTION (I): The research methodology project

95. This was an empirical project with rapporteurs for 27 Member States entrusted with the task of identifying competition case-law judgments in their national courts in the period between 1 May 1999 and 1 May 2012. The project focused on competition law judgments as opposed to whether any competition law claims had been filed,[10] and included all forms of case-law where competition law has been relied on rather than simply considering damages claims. Accordingly the project also sought to cover cases involving other remedies such as *inter alia* injunctions and declarations, whether contracts were null and void, and also 'defence' cases where the defendant relied on competition law in defence to some other form of civil law claim. The focus was on private enforcement case-law involving core competition law rules,[11] to the exclusion of case-law related to the state aid rules[12] or the Merger Regulation[13] and also litigation concerning aspects of the public enforcement process.[14] One enduring difficulty was ensuring consistency in the admittedly subjective task for each rapporteur in identifying whether a case materially concerned the application of the competition rules. Nonetheless, it should be stressed that rapporteurs were instructed to gather all case-law where a party pled competition law, even if the judgment itself was not a determination of the application of the substantive competition law rules in a final ruling, but for instance concerned the application of the limitation rules at an interim procedural

10 *Cf.* S. VAN de VALLE, *Private antitrust litigation in the European Union and Japan*, (Maklu, Antwerpen-Appeldoorn), 2013, in relation to the methodology used for identifying Japanese antitrust cases in Ch 6 'Empirical Analysis of Japanese Antitrust Cases' at pp. 128 et seq based on cases filed. See also the Ashurst Report, 'Study on the Conditions of Claims for damages in case of infringement of EC competition rules' (2004), available at http://ec.europa.eu/competition/antitrust/actionsdamages/comparative_report_clean_en.pdf, which was also based on 'judged cases'.

11 Article 101 and 102 TFEU and their domestic equivalent rules in the Member States. Even where either or both parties is a public body, for instance where a public body would sue for overpayment in relation to construction bid-rigging.

12 Articles 107-109 TFEU.

13 Council Regulation (EC) 139/2004, OJ 2004 L24/1.

14 For example where parties seek judicial review in relation to a competition authority infringement decision.

stage of the overall dispute.[15] The greatest difficulty generally across many of the Member States concerned identifying and locating all the relevant competition law case-law which would fall within the ambit of the project. Some competition law cases fail on a procedural issue or because of some other technical or legal hurdle and not simply because they have failed to establish the substantive competition law claim or defence to the requisite standard, but we considered it crucial to consider the purported application of competition law rights in a comprehensive manner. Much of the recent focus at European level has simply been on private damages actions. Whilst these are very important, and attract the highest public profile, it is important to recognise that competition law may also be used as a shield and that damages are not always an appropriate remedy for a competition law claimant. Moreover, it would provide merely a partial insight into competition litigation practice if one were only to consider and assess competition law rulings on the substance or merits after a trial (proof). This would ignore the wider legal framework in which competition law claims and defences may be successfully made and the context in which they are facilitated or obstructed. Accordingly, the research extends to all cases where competition law has been pled and relied on by either party, even where the ruling or judgment has not focused on the merits of the competition law issue itself, but may have determined a procedural aspect of the case. It is hoped that the research has been as comprehensive as possible.

96. One of the reasons for a methodological approach based on national rapporteurs from each Member State was the expectation that those national rapporteurs would understand the best way in their own legal system to locate the case-law as appropriate and to be as comprehensive as possible in that task. Nonetheless it is evident that this task was problematic in a number of States, and indeed there are inevitably some gaps in the final database of cases, and some missing data in a relatively small number of the final case-law sample.[16] It was agreed at an early stage of the research design process that Germany would be a particular and special case study as part of the overall project, partly because of the known methodological difficulties in dealing with cases over the full planned research period, and partly due to the volume of case-law which was anticipated. The aggregate EU data of 1268 cases, representing the aggregate

15 See the UK report in particular.
16 See in particular the Reports for Italy and Belgium.

of all cases EU-wide[17] exclude the German data, which cover a shorter period, and according to a slightly varied method of case-calculation. The German report covers the years 2004 to 2009 and, subject to some limitations, updates an earlier analysis of private enforcement of competition law.[18] The proceedings in the dataset were commenced mainly between 01 January 2004 and 31 December 2009. In relation to the case-law reporting task by the Member State rapporteurs, there were significant practical difficulties in certain jurisdictions in tracing relevant legal judgments within the project period.[19] This means that although this is the first time there has been an attempt to gather all competition case-law across the EU collectively over a particular time-frame, and in many Member States individually, it is clear that the data is not comprehensive[20] nor can the data provide completely accurate comparisons between Member States.

Section (II): Competition case-law across the EU

97. Within the timeframe of the project, the rapporteurs reported a total aggregate of 1268 competition law cases across the EU member States,[21] excluding Germany.[22] Of course this is likely to be a gross understatement of the total volume of competition law related litigation across the EU courts for two primary reasons. The first is the restricted scope of what constitutes competition law litigation for the purposes of this project – i.e. cases where Article 101, 102 TFEU or the national equivalents to Arts. 101 and 102 are pled and relied on by any of the parties to the litigation. The second is that for the purposes of this project, we use the terms 'cases' and 'case-law', and count the number of 'cases', solely by reference to available court judgments in disputes involving competition law, according to the methodology discussed above. Accordingly, omitted from the scope of the relevant case-law are any cases which settled prior to a

17 With the exception of the subsequent accession state of Croatia to the EU on 1 July 2013.

18 Sebastian Peyer, 'Private Antitrust Litigation in Germany from 2005 to 2007: Empirical Evidence' (2012) 8 Journal of Competition Law and Economics 331–359.

19 Both generally in locating relevant case-law, and, for instance in relation to Italy, in ascertaining specific aspects of the case-law.

20 Note the position in relation to Germany in particular, but there were also difficulties in other Member States, particularly Italy.

21 With the exception of Croatia, which joined the EU on 1 July 2013, after the research phase of the project had been finalised.

22 The case-law data for Germany is considered separately given the variation in period and case-law coverage by the German rapporteur.

court judgment,[23] and in a competition law context, this inevitably means that a considerable number of claims and disputes about which we may be aware in general, have to be ignored for our purposes.[24] Indeed, the data gathered evidences remarkably more case-law than had been previously imagined, even within the project limitations, and the reports from the Iberian rapporteurs for Spain and Portugal respectively indicate that the outcomes exceeded any prior expectations. Nonetheless, it should also be noted here that the case count is arguably over-inclusive in two ways. The first is that, unlike other attempts to chronicle private enforcement across the EU which have focused on damages actions alone,[25] this project counted as case-law any case where competition law has been pled by any party, whether in a damages claim or in an action for a declaration or injunction, or as a defence by the defendant – i.e. reliance on competition law in all its contexts. The second is that separate judgments each count as individual cases, and hence the same legal dispute may constitute various cases for the purposes of this research.[26] On the other hand, where a legal issue has been appealed and considered at different levels of the national court structure hierarchy, rapporteurs were instructed not to consider each court judgment but only to count the legal ruling by the highest court to decide on the issue within the project timescale. It is accepted that this leads to 'over-reporting' of appeal judgments and 'under-reporting' of first instance judgments. Furthermore, the methodological problems in locating and reporting case-law are likely to be exacerbated in the earlier years and therefore apparent increases in case-law in more recent periods may at least partly reflect enhanced case-law accessibility, partly due to improvements in national case-law databases. It should also be noted that the data for 2012 only represent case-law to 1 May 2012, and this should be borne in mind when assessing any trends or patterns in the case-law. Figure 1 sets out the aggregate data on competition law cases across the EU Member States' courts (excluding Germany) over the period of the research.

---

23 If there is a court judgment and then the parties settle the dispute, the court judgment counts as a 'case' for these purposes.

24 See B Rodger 'Private Enforcement of Competition Law, The Hidden story: Competition Litigation Settlements in the UK 2000-2005' [2008] European Competition Law Review pp. 96-116.

25 Notably the Ashurst Report, 'Study on the Conditions of Claims for damages in case of infringement of EC competition rules' (2004), available at http://ec.europa.eu/competition/antitrust/actionsdamages/comparative_report_clean_en.pdf.

26 For example, there may be judgments in the same legal dispute concerning limitation and later regarding quantification of damages or causation. The only way in which we could assess all the variables including success accurately was to treat each individual judgment as a case. This is particularly evident in relation to the UK report.

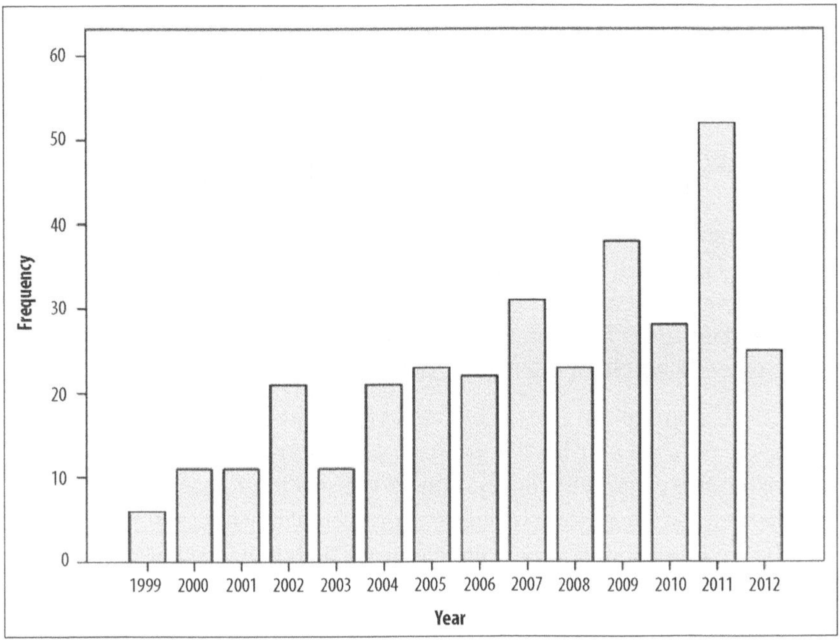

Figure 1: Aggregate EU cases per year

98. In relation to individual Member States, due to space constraints, it is necessary to focus on different sub-groups of Member States in relation to this central aspect of the research project.[27] It should also be stressed that only certain rapporteurs sought to identify and discuss the rationale for the levels of case-law in their jurisdiction. The case-law figures (with number of cases in brackets) for the 'May 2004 Accession States' are inevitably low, as follows: Bulgaria (0); Cyprus, Estonia and Latvia (1); Romania (3); Czech Republic (4); Lithuania, Slovakia and Slovenia (5);[28] and Poland (6). Perhaps unsurprisingly,[29] Hungary is the State in this group with the greatest number of case-law judgments with fifteen in total. In the second category of 'States with Limited Private Enforcement Experience', we have

27 For the purposes of the project, the following categories were established: – *May 2004 Accession States*; *States with Limited Private Enforcement Experience*; *States with Developing Private Enforcement Experience* and *States with Considerable Private Enforcement Experience*.

28 Although note that one of the Slovakian cases was a pre-accession case.

29 See for instance, C. I. Nagy, 'The new Hungarian rules on damages caused by horizontal hardcore cartels: presumed price increase and limited protection for whistleblowers—an analytical introduction' [2011] ECLR 32(2) 63-67.

Finland (4); Luxembourg (4) and Malta (7).The third tier of countries, 'States with Developing Private Enforcement Practice', includes Austria (64); Denmark (10); Greece (27); Ireland (24); Portugal (24);[30] and Sweden (25).[31]

States with Considerable Private Enforcement Experience

99. Inevitably in this article we will focus on this sub-set of States, where the reported case-law reflected the anticipation that we would observe greater levels of competition law judgments.[32] This group includes (in alphabetical order): Belgium (128); France (71); Germany;[33] Italy (98);[34] the Netherlands (308); Spain (323); and the UK (106).

100. In this group of States in particular, due to the higher level of reported cases, we may be able to observe similar patterns and/or distinctive national trends, both in relation to the levels of case-law judgments but also in relation to the other case-law variables which the rapporteurs required to report on in spreadsheets for each Member State.[35] In this section, we shall review the position for each State in alphabetical order, but because of the special position of Germany in the research project, it shall be considered last.

101. The Belgian case-law (128 cases) is evidently fairly steady through the first ten years but appears to have tailed off since 2009 (with only 9 and 4 judgments in 2010 and 2011 respectively). The French rapporteurs note that private enforcement in France is not as "underdeveloped" as it may have been described[36] and the French courts have ruled on a significant

30 The Portuguese and Irish case-law experience is similar, with the same number of judgments overall. The Portuguese rapporteurs stressed in their report that the research outcomes would surprise many Portuguese academics and practitioners, with considerably more case-law than anticipated.

31 The Swedish experience in terms of number of cases is similar to that in Ireland and Portugal although a recent rise to 3 and 4 cases in 2010 and 2011 may indicate a possible upward future trend.

32 It is accepted that the placing of particular Member States within these categories was arbitrary, and it is notable that the case-law frequency in Austria and France appears to be similar, although the difficulties in case identification in particular in the former suggest that there are considerably more cases in that jurisdiction. Furthermore, at the outset of the project it was considered that Spain was likely to be in the 'States with Developing private Enforcement Experience' category.

33 See discussion below regarding the German cases dataset, over a considerably shorter period than 1999-2012.

34 This clearly understates the true picture of private enforcement case-law in Italy.

35 The rapporteurs provided the case data on an excel spreadsheet but the data was subsequently transferred to SPSS (20) for data analysis and generation of tables and charts.

36 See Ashurst Report 2004, *supra* n° 26.

number of claims, counterclaims and defences based on competition law. The review of collected cases shows that in many cases, contractors used competition law in the context of contractual disputes, and the preponderance of competition law defences is notable, although competition law has also been used in the absence of any contractual relationship between the claimant and defendant in the action.

102. The data collected for Italy shows that private enforcement of competition law in Italy is well-developed and national and EU competition rules have been frequently applied by the courts. In the period 1999-2012 the number of final judgments on competition law cases for this project was 98.[37] Nonetheless, this number does not take into account the extensive follow-on litigation related to the Car Insurance cartel that gave rise alone (in the period 2000-2012) to more than one hundred thousand individual actions.[38] Even excluding the impact of that litigation, the quantitative dimension of private competition law enforcement in Italy is impressive taking into account that: i) the National Competition Act is relatively new (it was enacted in 1990) and ii) end consumers have been entitled only very recently (in 2005) to bring judicial actions based on national competition law provisions.[39] Moreover it must be taken into account that the Italian judicial system lacks *ad hoc* procedural mechanisms aimed at making it easier for victims of competition law violations to bring legal actions in court, although in 2009 a new procedural tool available to end consumers was introduced: the collective action (*azione di classe*).[40]

103. In the Netherlands, the number of civil competition law cases is relatively high in comparison to most other EU member states. On average, each year circa 20 competition law cases are decided in the Netherlands, with over 300 civil court decisions in private enforcement competition law cases found during the research period (308). Private competition law enforcement by consumers is rare in the Netherlands. In the reporting period, only a few cases were brought before the civil courts involving consumers (or consumer organisations). The majority of the civil competition cases in the Netherlands relate to the compatibility of (distribution) agreements. The main recurring theme in these cases is whether a supplier is obliged to (continue to) accept distributors in its distribution network.

[37] Of course, as the rapporteur stressed, this is not an official case count and the level of case-law may vary according to the criteria used to measure it.

[38] According to public information available.

[39] Legal standing for end consumers was established by the Supreme Court (*Corte di Cassazione*) by decision n° 2207, February 4th 2005.

[40] See art. 140*bis*, D. Lgs N° 206/2005.

Since 2010 there has been a rise in cartel damages claims as a 'follow on' from cartel decisions by the European Commission. Many of these claims are pursued by special purpose claim vehicles that have bought/gathered the claims from various companies, and these have only recently started to find their way to the Dutch courts. Currently, private litigation is pending following on the Commission's decisions on gas-insulated switchgear,[41] bitumen,[42] air cargo,[43] sodium chlorate,[44] candle waxes[45] and elevator and escalator[46] sectors. With the exception of the decision in the electro-technical fittings cartel,[47] not many of these cases have progressed (much) beyond preliminary procedural decisions.

104. The rapporteur explained that the evidence produced in the Spanish report challenges the traditional view that private litigation in Spain is underdeveloped, amounting only to a few noted cases. The number of cases reported here (323) suggests otherwise: there are many more private claims than previously thought, making the Spanish experience somehow comparable to that of certain other EU Member States. The longstanding concern over the under-development and lack of significance of competition law private litigation in Spain should now be disregarded: since 2004 more than twenty cases per year decide claims based on competition law, and that number has been more than doubled in 2011 and 2012. The upsurge may possibly be attributed to the creation of the new commercial courts in 2004,[48] with powers to decide on the enforcement of articles 101 and 102 TFEU.[49] However, the trends of competition litigation in each industry may well be explained by specific factors (distinct strategic and legal reasons).

---

41 Commission Decision 24 January 2007, Case COMP/38899.

42 Commission Decision 13 September 2006, Case COMP/38456.

43 Commission Decision 9 November 2010, Case COMP/39258.

44 Commission Decision 11 June 2008, Case COMP/38695.

45 Commission Decision 1 October 2008, Case COMP/39181.

46 Commission Decision 21 February 2007, Case COMP/38823.

47 Commission Decision 26 October 1999, Case IV/33.884. See District Court Rotterdam 7 March 2007, *LJN* BA0926.

48 On the circumstances surrounding their creation (and especially referring to their powers in enforcing EU Regulation 1/2003), see Juan M. Fernández López, "Los juzgados de lo mercantil ante el Derecho Comunitario de la Competencia", *Anuario de la Competencia 2003*, pp. 172-180.

49 Article 86ter.2.f) of the Organic Law on Judicial Power. See Official Journal n° 164, 10 July 2003, pp. 26901-26905. However, only competence to decide EU cases was given to commercial courts, whilst domestic competition law cases were still to be decided by ordinary civil courts, as noted by the Ashurst, *Comparative Report* (Waelbroeck, Slater & Even-Shoshan), 2004, *supra* n° 67 p. 33 and also Mª Jesús González López, "La aplicación privada de las normas de competencia en España y su regulación en la Ley 15/2007", *ADI*, vol. 28 (2008) pp. 270-272. For that reason, see Provincial Court of Madrid (Sect. 28) Decree of 5th June 2009, *Spain Rail v. ADIF, Renfe-Operadora & Transportes Carrasco* (EDJ 2009/2622254) and Provincial

105. In the UK, there have been 106 judgments overall in the relevant period, in 80 separate disputes, as there have been judgments in relation to different aspects of the same dispute in some cases.[50] Some cases, particularly through the CAT avenue, have been legal sagas with multiple judgments on various issues. In terms of background to the UK data, earlier research demonstrated a slow but significant increase in the rate of cases through the 1970s, 1980s and 1990s. Nonetheless, the relatively frequent airing of competition law issues during the 1980s, and the 1970s in particular, may come as a surprise. Litigants started to use the competition law provisions fairly early following the UK's accession to the European Union, and there are a number of interesting cases in these early periods, although the resort to the competition law provisions as a Euro-defence, particularly by defendants in IP infringement cases, is fairly notable. There has been an increase in case-law judgments, and anecdotal evidence is that there had been a considerable increase in private litigation over the past ten years, with the majority of cases settling,[51] and considerable on-going litigation in the High Court in relation to a number of major international cartels.[52] More recently, although formally outside the temporal scope of the project, the award of over £33k (plus interest) in lost profit, and perhaps more significantly, an additional award of £60k for exemplary damages in *2 Travel Group PLC (in Liquidation) v Cardiff City Transport Services Ltd*[53] is the first successful, final award of damages by the CAT – and was followed by a subsequent £1.6m damages award in March 2013 in *Albion Water v Dwr Cymru Cyfyngedig.*[54] It is clear that due to the

Court of Barcelona (Sect. 17) Judgment of 19th March 2010, *Necchi Blu System v: Necchi Modulare Música España* (EDJ 2010/154105). On that issue – but noting the beneficial effects of assigning private damages claims based on competition violations to these newly created courts – see Diego Castro-Villacañas Pérez, "La aplicación privada del Derecho de competencia y los nuevos juzgados de lo mercantil", Boletín Económico del ICE nº 2818 (2004) pp. 8-10.

50 Although this figure has clearly been affected by the rationale for exclusion of a number of cases which initially appeared following the searches. It should also be noted that where a case has been appealed, it is only referred to once and in some instances in a subsequent year.

51 Of course, one must always be aware of the 'hidden story' of competition litigation settlements which ensures that the visible litigation practice is effectively the 'tip of the iceberg':- See B. Rodger, 'Private Enforcement of Competition Law, The Hidden Story: Competition Litigation Settlements in the UK 2000-2005' [2008] ECLR 96.

52 B. Rodger, 'Why not court? A study of follow-on actions in the UK' (2013) 1(1) Journal of Antitrust Enforcement 104-131.

53 *2 Travel Group PLC (in Liquidation) v Cardiff City Transport Services Ltd* [2012] CAT 19. It is anticipated that there will be considerable academic literature on the CAT ruling in 2 Travel Group plc, but at this stage, see http://competitionpolicy.wordpress.com/2012/07/23/cardiff-bus-exemplary-damages-in-follow-on-cases/ and C. Veljanovski, 'CAT Awards Triple Damages, Well Not Really – Cardiff Bus, and the Dislocation between Liability and Damages for Exclusionary Abuse' [2012] ECLR 47-49.

54 [2013] CAT 6.

prevalence of settlement activity, the published judgments represent only a partial view of competition litigation strategy in the UK.[55] There is some evidence, as noted, of a recent increase in the number of claims being raised before the CAT, and it has delivered some important judgments to date, although to date these have tended to be procedural skirmishes related to time-bar, costs and jurisdiction, but the consumer representative claim provision is clearly not an appropriate mechanism to incentivise 'class actions'. It may be that the profile associated with the very recent, successful damages awards in *2 Travel Group PLC (in Liquidation) v Cardiff City Transport Services Ltd and Albion Water v Dwr Cymru Cyfyngedig* may increase awareness of the possibility to seek redress for aggrieved parties, and thereby encourage follow-on claims, particularly before the CAT. Collective redress in particular may also be facilitated by the proposals made by BIS in 2013, introduced in the draft Consumer Rights Bill, to extend the scope of the jurisdiction of the CAT and introduce opt-out collective actions before the CAT.[56]

106. The German data, as alluded to earlier, for methodological and logistical reasons, could not cover the full period, and the proceedings covered in the dataset were commenced mainly between 01 January 2004 and 31 December 2009. There are a number of legal, institutional and cultural reasons which have ensured that private enforcement is at such a high level in Germany, primarily the absence of litigation costs disincentives and cultural aversion to litigation, allied with the accumulation of repeat-player knowledge and experience of competition litigation strategies by legal experts in that legal system.

Section (III): Remedies in competition litigation

107. Rapporteurs were asked to classify cases in relation to a number of issues (such as the level of court at which the judgment was made; whether it was a follow-on or stand-alone action; the stage of the proceedings at which the judgment was delivered; the competition law provisions relied upon in the case, and whether the case was successful) and this article concentrates on the issue of the remedies sought for each case.

55 B. Rodger, 'The Hidden Story.' [2008] ECLR *supra* n° 54.

56 See https://www.gov.uk/government/publications/draft-consumer-rights-bill.

108. For the purposes of this project,[57] the remedy sought is considered purely from the perspective of the party pleading competition law. In order to emphasise that this project was not simply focused on competition law damages actions, and concerned the exercise of rights afforded by competition law more generally, various options in terms of the 'remedy' sought by the party pleading competition law rules were available to the rapporteurs in categorising cases: Damages; Injunction; Defence; Declaration; Pre-action Disclosure; Damages and other remedy; and Other combination. Accordingly, if the case involves a claimant relying on competition law, the remedy may be an injunction or damages or a declaration, but in many cases it may be the defendant who raises the competition law issue as a defence, and in such a case 'defence' would be the option utilised.[58] Table 1 and Figure 2 provide the aggregated EU data in relation to remedies sought, with the exception of Germany.[59]

Table 1 – Aggregate EU cases remedies sought

REMEDIES SOUGHT		Frequency	Valid Percent	Cumulative Percent
	Damages	213	17.1	17.1
	Injunction	342	27.4	44.5
	Defence	309	24.8	69.3
	Declaration	128	10.3	79.6
	Pre-action disclosure	12	1.0	80.6
	Damages and other Remedy	173	13.9	94.5
	Other Combination	69	5.5	100.0
	Total	1246	100.0	
	Missing	22		
Total		1268		

57 And see earlier similar work focusing on the UK only by the author: – B. Rodger, 'Competition Law Litigation in the UK Courts: A Study of All Cases to 2004 – Part I'[2006] ECLR 241; 'Competition Law Litigation in the UK Courts: A Study of All Cases to 2004 – Part II' [2006] ECLR 279; 'Competition Law Litigation in the UK Courts: A Study of All Cases to 2004 – Part III' [2006] ECLR 341. See also B Rodger, 'Competition law litigation in the UK courts: a study of all cases 2005-2008 – Part I' (2009) Global Competition Litigation Review, 93-114; Part II, 136-147 and B. Rodger 'Competition law Litigation in the UK Courts: A Study of all Cases 2009-2012' [2013] 6/2 GCLR 55-67.

58 Note that with hindsight nullity should have been given a separate category, though nullity cases are virtually always either a declaration or a defence, or combined with damages (particularly in relation to Germany).

59 Note for some cases the remedy sought could not be identified by certain rapporteurs – twenty two cases in this instance, and accordingly the (valid) percentages set out in the Table are based on the remaining cases.

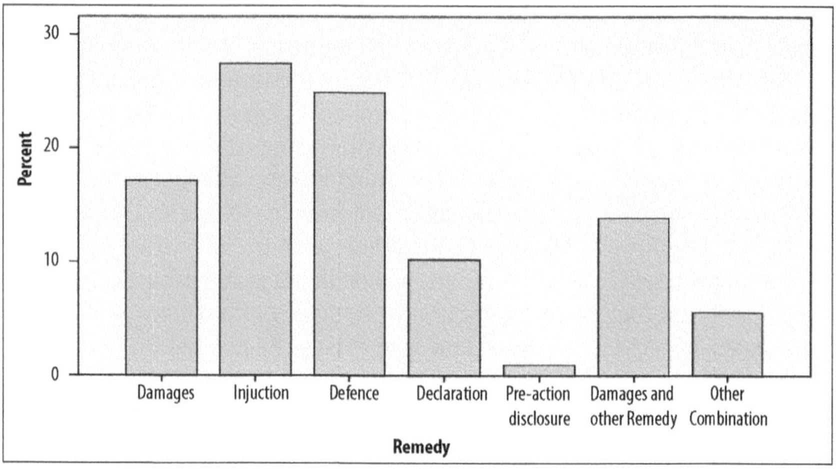

Figure 2: Aggregate EU cases remedies sought

109. It is very interesting to note here the frequency of 'injunction' cases, at 27.4% of the total. Together with the significant figure of 24.8% 'defence' cases, these 2 categories alone make up a sizeable majority of the total competition case-law, and when added to 'declaration' cases (10.3%), the figure of non-damages cases stands at (at least)[60] 62.5%, whereas 'damages' claims constitute only 17.1% of the total and 31% when combined with 'damages and other remedy' cases.[61] This outcome alone underlines the rationale for the research being extended to include non-damages cases as otherwise we would ignore a significant level of case-law in which the national courts have been called upon to adjudicate on the rights afforded to parties as a result of infringements of either domestic or EU competition law rules. There is a varied picture in relation to the provisions relied upon and remedies sought across the Member States.

1. May 2004 Accession States and States with Limited Private Enforcement Experience

110. There is very little experience in either of these first two groups and therefore the main focus will be on the other two groupings of States. In

60 'Other combination' cases may or may not include damages claims.

61 It was also noted that a significantly lower proportion of 'injunction' cases were decided at appeal level, (50.9%) compared to the figures for the two other principal remedies, damages (60.1%) and defences (66%).

Poland, none of the cases were damages claims and all essentially focused on the nullity of contract issue such that private enforcement in Poland has to date played the role of 'shield' rather than 'sword'. Apart from one case concerned with an anti-competitive agreement, the case-law has concerned abuse of a dominant position (the domestic rule), and this can be related to the period of transformation of the Polish economy. Similarly, five of the Maltese cases were defence cases.

2. States with Developing Private Enforcement Experience

111. In Denmark, where all ten cases have involved the application of the domestic competition law rules,[62] the majority of cases (6) were damages claims, and these tend to be follow-on claims. Similarly, of the twenty seven Greece cases twenty three were damages actions alone. In Austria, an exceptionally high figure of 65.6% of all Austrian case-law involved injunctions, with considerably lower levels of case-law for all the remaining categories of remedies compared to the EU wide aggregate, as demonstrated by Figure 3.

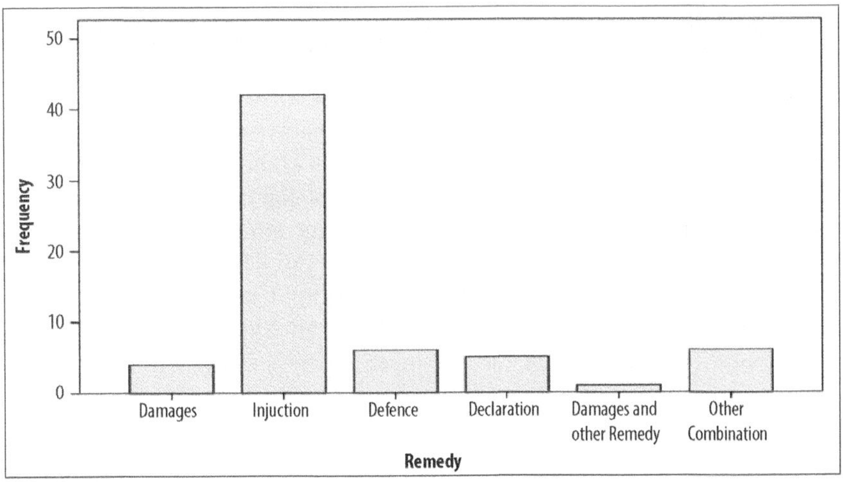

Figure 3: Austria cases remedies sought

[62] Six involving the Article 101 domestic equivalent rule and two involving the Article 102 domestic equivalent rule, with only two cases at least partially involving the application of the EU rules (Article 102 and the domestic equivalent rule).

112. These figures for Austria may be explicable by a combination of the remedies available and the courts competent to deal with competition law claims. Only the ordinary civil courts can deal with damages claims and the nullity defence[63] and less than one third of the total Austrian case-law for the period derives from civil court cases – although the rapporteur notes a clear trend towards increasing numbers of damages claims in recent years which is likely to continue. The specialist Cartel Court on the other hand, which has dealt with the vast majority of competition law cases, has exclusive jurisdiction to grant injunctions, and also declarations.[64] Most of the injunction cases involved alleged infringements solely of Art 102 and/or its Austrian equivalent, and accordingly, perhaps unsurprisingly, this specific remedy by a specialist court has usually been sought by undertakings in order to protect them from an (at least allegedly) abusive behaviour of another (usually larger or more aggressive) undertaking.

113. The vast majority of cases in Portugal were defence cases (62.5%) and this reflected the common incidence of case-law involving the vertical relations between manufacturers and distributors or retailers. A particular set of national data comes from Sweden, where the most common remedy sought has been injunctions (in 44% of the cases). Some background to the Swedish legal context may help us to understand this phenomenon. Of particular interest for private enforcement is the rule on the subsidiary right to litigate outlined in chapter 2, section 2 of the Swedish Competition Act. It stipulates that if the KKV decides in a particular case not to impose injunctions, the Market Court may do so at the request of an undertaking that is affected by the infringement. This right is restricted insofar as it cannot be used if the KKV is basing its decision on Article 13 of the Council Regulation 1/2003. The subsidiary claim appears to be intended as a safeguard against the effects arising out of the KKV failing to fulfil its task, regardless of the reason of failure, based upon budgetary constraints, lack of staff, misjudgement in law etc. In practice, the subsidiary right can be an important instrument for aggrieved parties, at least in cases when competitor and competition concerns coincide. The majority of private litigation cases in Sweden have in fact been subsidiary claims for injunctions. A subsidiary claim does not entail any compensation for the suffering parties, but it addresses the heart of the problem as it is directed towards

63 In addition to injunction suits.

64 To declare that (i) an infringement has been committed in the past if there is a legitimate interest in doing so, and/or (ii) to declare whether certain facts fall at all within the scope of the Austrian competition law regime.

prohibited behaviour. Frequently, this appears to be sufficient, and to date there have been no follow-on cases for damages subsequent to the Market Court findings of e.g. abuse of dominance resulting in an injunction.

3. States with Considerable Private Enforcement Experience

114. For Belgium, injunction cases again predominate but with a significantly higher frequency than across the EU, with 45.3% of the total. The figures for defence and declaration cases are also higher than for the EU aggregate at 31.6% and 15.4%. This means that only 3.4% of cases are damages only and in combination with the damages and other remedy category (4.3%) only 7.7% of the competition case-law in Belgium has involved a party seeking damages. Private enforcement of the competition rules mainly occurs 'deviously' – according to the rapporteur –, via the rules on unfair competition and in particular by means of the cessation action. A cessation action before the civil courts is not provided by the Belgian Competition Act as a private remedy for an infringement of the competition rules themselves. It is only indirectly available, by interposition of unfair competition law. The Act on Commercial Practices and Consumer Protection was replaced by the 2011 Act (April 6th) on Market Practices and Consumer Protection (WMPC[65]) and an Act of the same date on Certain Procedures relating to the WMPC, in particular the cessation action.[66] According to the Belgian rapporteur, because of the swiftness of this procedure, not only compared to other civil actions, but also as compared to the process following a complaint to the national competition authority, it is very popular. When an undertaking considers itself aggrieved by the anti-competitive practices of another undertaking, a cessation action will normally be its first choice. Follow-on actions are therefore very rare. With the exception of four cases where an interim injunction was sought,[67] all actions for injunctions brought in Belgium are cessation actions. However,

65 Wet 6 april 2010 betreffende de marktpraktijken en de consumentenbescherming, *Belgian Official Journal* 12 April 2010.

66 A cessation action for conduct which harms or may harm the professional interests of one or more undertakings is now available on the basis of Art. 95 WMPC *juncto* Art. 2 Act of 6 April 2011 on Certain Procedures relating to the WMPC.

67 Pres. Comm. Brussels 12 February 2002 (Sourcepower SA/Elia SA) (interim measures), *JLMB* 2002, 1146; Pres. Civil Court of First Instance Brussels 23 June 2005 (Pay TV CO NV and BeTV NV/Liga Beroepsvoetbal VZW) (interim measures), *Jaarboek Handelspraktijken & Mededinging* 2005, 983; Pres. Comm. Liège 23 April 2007 (Green Cycle Associates AB et al./ SA Amaury Sports Organisation) (interim measures), http://ec.europa.eu/competition/elojade/

comparing the number of cessation actions with that of other remedies, it seems that the former is losing its predominant role as a means for the private enforcement of competition law. The importance of the cessation action as a means for the private enforcement of competition law seems to have decreased during the second half of the period under investigation. Damages actions have been rare and only one of these cases, the most typical cartel damages claim, was a follow-on case. The number of defences is higher during the second half of the period under investigation. Defences have rarely been successful in Belgium, although their success rate increased during the second half of the period.

115. In France, the rapporteurs stress that private enforcement concerns not only damages claims, but also other remedies such as the invalidity of agreements, and injunctions. Nonetheless, damages claims clearly predominate with 53.5% of cases being damages claims alone (added to the 4.2% of damages and other remedy cases to make 57.7%), although there is also a significant minority of defence cases in this jurisdiction at 21.1% of the total case-law. The rapporteurs note that the collected case-law shows that in many cases, contractors have used competition law in the context of contractual disputes.

116. In Italy, as demonstrated by Table 2, damages actions, primarily in relation to the domestic prohibitions, predominate. Damages actions alone constituted 47.1% of the total cases;[68] and together with damages and other remedy cases amounted to 57.4%. Indeed 35.5% (36 of the relevant 87 cases) were damages actions based on either of the domestic infringements, although it is notable, and perhaps unsurprising, that 12 of the 17 injunction cases involved the domestic Article 102 infringement.

antitrust/nationalcourts/?ms_code=bel.; Comm. Brussels 3 September 2009 (GS1 Hellas SA/GS1 ASBL) (interim measures), *Jaarboek Handelspraktijken & Mededinging* 2009, 1052.

68 Note for some cases the remedy sought could not be identified by the rapporteur – eleven cases in this instance, and accordingly the (valid) percentages set out in the Table are based on the remaining cases.

Table 2 – Italy cases remedies sought

REMEDIES SOUGHT		Frequency	Valid Percent	Cumulative Percent
	Damages	41	47.1	47.1
	Injunction	17	19.5	66.7
	Declaration	5	5.7	72.4
	Damages and other Remedy	9	10.3	82.8
	Other Combination	15	17.2	100.0
	Total	87	100.0	
	Missing	11		
Total		98		

117. From the Netherlands data, there is a predominance of injunctions actions (55.8%-172 cases) with a correspondingly very small proportion of damages cases (2.6%-8 cases, increasing to 3.2%-10 cases including the damages and other remedy category). The fairly high level of defences is notable (24.4%-75 cases), though unsurprisingly most common in domestic Art 101 cases (35 cases). Most interesting is that although there is, as would be anticipated, a fairly high level of injunctions in abuse cases (for instance 28 in domestic Article 102 cases), 75 of the 172 injunction cases (43.6%) involved the domestic Article 101 equivalent prohibition.

Table 3 – Netherlands cases remedies sought

REMEDIES SOUGHT		Frequency	Percent	Cumulative Percent
	Damages	8	2.6	2.6
	Injunction	172	55.8	58.4
	Defence	75	24.4	82.8
	Declaration	21	6.8	89.6
	Damages and other Remedy	2	.6	90.3
	Other Combination	30	9.7	100.0
Total		308	100.0	

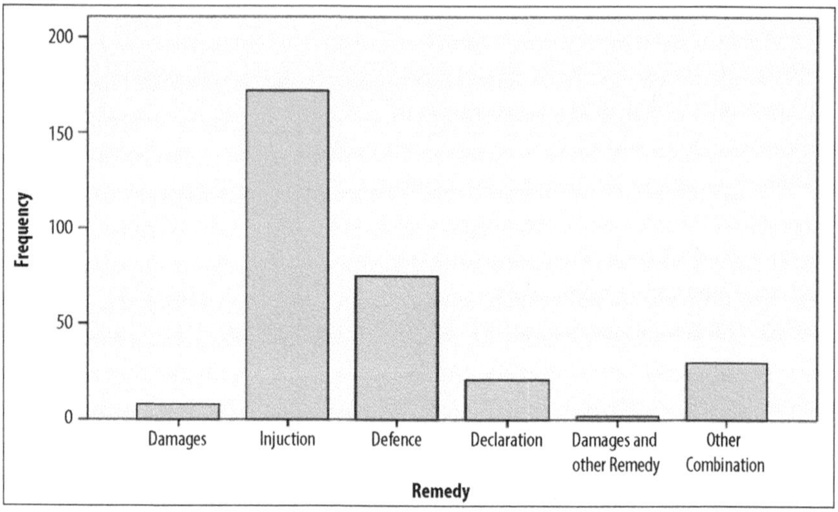

Figure 4: Netherlands cases remedies sought

118. Two contextual factors are key here as stressed by the rapporteur. The first is that over half of the cases involved distribution agreements. The main recurring theme in these cases is whether a supplier was obliged to (continue to) accept distributors in its distribution network. The second is that nearly half of the competition law cases encountered were decided in summary proceedings: of the 308 cases found in the reporting period, 141 were summary proceedings. Summary proceedings are quick proceedings in which injunctive relief may be claimed and the ordinary rules of evidence do not apply in such proceedings and accordingly they are used routinely in the Dutch legal system, which may at least partly account for the frequency with which injunctive relief has been sought.

119. The Spanish data demonstrates that the figures for defence (32.5%) and declaration (17.6%) cases is significantly higher than the EU aggregate, with correspondingly fewer damages and injunction cases (at 4.3% each of the total). The Spanish rapporteur explained the background to competition litigation on an industry-by-industry basis and identified trends of competition litigation in each industry which may well be explained by specific factors (distinct strategic and legal reasons). Given that the competition law claim is frequently just complementary or secondary to other legal arguments (mainly based on contract law), both when used as a "sword" and as a "shield" by litigants, there exists considerable strategic use (or misuse) of competition law arguments. Almost all of the claims reported in the database concern business to business claims (B2B), and there is only one consumer to business claim (C2B). Most of the claims refer to contractual disputes in vertical relationships in which competition law is raised (either by the claimant or defendant) as a ground for nullity and/or damages. Vertical relations involve almost two thirds of the private disputes so far. Most of the cases concern litigation between petrol station retailers and their providers (49%).[69] Distribution contracts in other sectors amount to 10% of the cases. The case-law reported here challenges the view that private enforcement of competition law mainly has a compensatory aim. Although claimants have asked for damages as compensation in some of the claims reported, damages awards have been rare so far. The most frequent outcome reached in successful claims is a declaration of a violation and nullity/voidness of anti-competitive clauses in contracts.

120. Again the picture in the UK is dramatically different and reflective of the legal avenues and redress available within the legal systems of the UK and the interplay of the relevant legal provisions and remedies available. The data on remedies sought, as set out in Table 4, is considerably different from the EU picture with an emphasis on damages (42.5%), considerably less injunction cases (14.2% compared to the EU aggregate of 27.4%) but with a comparable number of defence cases (25.5% to the EU aggregate 24.9%).

Table 4 – UK cases remedies sought

REMEDY SOUGHT	Frequency	Percent	Cumulative Percent
Damages	45	42.5	42.5
Injunction	15	14.2	56.6
Defence	27	25.5	82.1
Declaration	5	4.7	86.8
Pre-action disclosure	2	1.9	88.7
Damages and other Remedy	12	11.3	100.0
Total	106	100.0	

[69] Indeed some commentators talk about the "petrol stations saga". See F. Marcos, 'Filling the tank of antitrust private enforcement in Spain: why are there so many judicial claims in the retail fuel industry?' WP IE Law School, September 2013.

121. Taking the latter first, it is evident over the period of the research that the use of competition law as a defence, either in an abuse or anti-competitive agreement context, has been decreasing relative to other remedies in recent years,[70] and this is a common phenomenon with other Member States, as damages actions in particular have been increasing. Although injunctions, and interlocutory injunctions, have been available, and successful in some notable instances,[71] historically it has been difficult to succeed in an interlocutory injunction claim, and this may have made parties reluctant to proceed in this context.[72] The level, and recent increase, in damages actions can at least be partly explained by the availability of the follow-on damages (only) mechanism before the CAT, and although there is still considerable competition damages litigation before the High Court,[73] there has been extensive case-law (by the CAT and Court of Appeal) in relation to aspects of this mechanism. As outlined in the UK report,[74] although there have been considerable case judgments, including multiple judgments on different legal aspects of the dispute in certain cases, and many are classified as 'damages' actions, it is only more recently that there have actually been damages awards,[75] despite the formal classification of a significant number of 'damages' cases as successful. Although some of the follow-on damages cases have involved domestic Article 102 infringements, the vast majority of follow-on cases have related to cartel infringement findings by the European Commission under Article 101.[76]

122. In relation to remedies sought, the German rapporteur notes that results are restricted to the primarily sought remedy. In some instances, claimants ask for more than one remedy. Typically, a claimant seeks an

70 See B. Rodger, 'Competition Law Litigation in the UK Courts: A Study of All Cases to 2004 – Part I'[2006] ECLR 241; 'Competition Law Litigation in the UK Courts: A Study of All Cases to 2004 – Part II' [2006] ECLR 279; 'Competition Law Litigation in the UK Courts: A Study of All Cases to 2004 – Part III' [2006] ECLR 341.

71 See for example *Purple Parking Ltd v Heathrow Airport Ltd* [2011] EWHC 987 (Ch).

72 See A. MacCulloch and B. Rodger, 'Wielding the Blunt Sword: Interim Relief for Breaches of EC Competition Law before the UK Courts' [1996] E.C.L.R. 393. *Cf.* B. Rodger, 'Early Steps to a Mature Competition Law System; Case Law Developments in the First Eighteen Months of the Competition Act 1998', [2002] 2 ECLR *pp. 52*-67 and see also for instance the discussion *in* B. Rodger, 'UK competition law and private litigation' Ch 3 in B Rodger (ed.) *Ten Years of UK Competition Law Reform* (DUP, 2010).

73 See B. Rodger, 'Why not court? A study of follow-on actions in the UK' Journal of Antitrust Enforcement (2013) 1(1) 104-131.

74 See also B. Rodger, 'Competition law Litigation in the UK Courts: A Study of all Cases 2009-2012' [2013] 6/2 GCLR 55-67.

75 *2 Travel Group PLC (in Liquidation) v Cardiff City Transport Services Ltd* [2012] CAT 19 and *Albion Water v Dwr Cymru Cyfyngedig*,[2013] CAT 6.

76 See B. Rodger, 'Why not Court' supra n74.

injunction to stop the anti-competitive conduct and, subsequently, sues for damages. It is likely that claimants prefer to establish the infringement before they proceed with a damages action. Thus, reporting only the primary remedy creates a bias against damages actions, and monetary relief may be underreported. The primary remedy is known for 607 cases of the total of 608 proceedings. Table 5 gives an overview about the various types of claims. Damages are one of the remedies that claimants seek less often (in the first place). Although the dataset reports few claims aimed at compensation, it seems that firms are increasingly aware of the possibility of follow-on damages claims against cartelists.[77] While the rare occurrence of damages actions may support the hypothesis that consumers and firms lack a suitable framework for redress, monetary demands can also be satisfied by unjust enrichment claims. The data show that 14 per cent of all primary remedies are unjust enrichment claims brought for the violation of competition law. These claims provide pecuniary relief if the parties transferred money or goods between them and this transfer (contract) is null and void because it fell afoul of completion law. Claimants most frequently employ injunction claims, i.e. court orders to stop or prevent unlawful behaviour. In more than 40 per cent of the antitrust actions this was the case. In some instances an injunction may also be the first remedy that, if successful, leads to a damages action. Claimants sought an interim injunction in 121 proceedings; these are almost 50 per cent of all injunction claims. According to section 33(1) ARC, victims may seek a permanent injunction against repeated, imminent or on-going anticompetitive conduct.[78] The ARC of 1957 already provided for injunctive relief, i.e. the right to ask the defendant to refrain from repeated breaches or an imminent violation of competition law. The 7th amendment of 2005 expanded the injunction claim adding a so-called removal claim to deal with on-going infringements.[79] This latter type of claim is not new but it was derived from statutory provisions in the Civil Code.[80] Professional associations

77 BGH of 28 June 2011, KZR 75/10, NJW 2012, 928, *ORWI*; KG of 01 October 2009, 2 U 10/03 Kart and 2 U 17/03; OLG München of 09 February 2012, U 3283/11 Kart; LG Mannheim of 04 May 2012, 7 O 436/11 Kart and 7 O 436/11, *Feuerwehrlöschfahrzeuge*.

78 See Peyer, 'Injunctive Relief and Private Antitrust Enforcement' (2011) CCP Working Paper n° 11-7. Available at SSRN: http://ssrn.com/abstract=1861861.

79 For an overview see Alexander Fritzsche, 'Der Beseitigungsanspruch im Kartellrecht nach der 7. GWB-Novelle, Zugleich ein Beitrag zur Dogmatik des quasi-negatorischen Beseitigungsanspruchs' (2006) Wettbewerb in Recht und Praxis 42–54; Jörg Fritzsche, *Unterlassungsanspruch und Unterlassungsklage* (Springer, Berlin 2007).

80 Volker Emmerich in Ulrich Immenga and Ernst-Joachim Mestmäcker (eds), *GWB: Kommentar zum Deutschen Kartellrecht* (4th edn Beck, München 2007) § 33 para 90. See section 1004(1)1 Civil Code.

representing a number of undertakings can seek an injunction on behalf of their members pursuant to section 33(2) ARC if the conduct in question violates the interest of their members. If time is of the essence, claimants may file for an interim injunction. Interim relief is granted according to section 935 of the Civil Procedure Code.

Table 5 – Germany primary claim in cases

Claim	*Frequency*	*Per cent of total*
Injunction	250	41.19
Nullity	180	29.65
Restitution	87	14.33
Damages	46	7.58
Other*	44	7.25
Total	607	100

* Other includes request for information, declaration of infringements etc.

123. Table 5 reveals that claimants asked the courts in almost one third of the cases to void a contract or contract clause. Nullity requests have a reputation for being used in contractual disputes by the initial defendant to alter a binding agreement. The data confirm that the vast majority of those claims, 141 out of 180, are actually counterclaims.

Section (IV): Remedies and other data

124. Having looked at the position in relation to the EU and key Member States in relation to the remedies sought it is also instructive to analyse the cross-tabulated data between the provisions relied upon and remedies sought to ascertain if there are any particular patterns in the case-law and similarities or differences in those patterns across the Member States. The aggregated EU cross-tabulation between provisions relied upon and remedies sought are set out in Table 6.

Table 6 – Aggregate EU cases cross-tabulation provision/remedy

PROVISION RELIED UPON	REMEDY SOUGHT							Total
	Damages	Injunction	Defence	Declaration	Pre-action disclosure	Damages and other Remedy	Other Combination	
Art. 101	46	28	74	34	1	77	19	279
Art. 102	6	17	14	6	1	6	4	54
Domestic Art. 101	49	91	81	33	0	15	9	278
Domestic Art. 102	54	106	33	18	1	21	15	248
Art. 101 and Domestic	21	12	49	13	0	31	1	127
Art. 102 and Domestic	15	21	17	6	2	11	5	77
Combination	22	67	41	18	7	12	16	183
Total	213	342	310	127	12	173	69	1246

125. It can be observed that the damages remedy is spread fairly consistently across the range of competition law provisions,[81] but in relation to Article 101, the damages remedy alone constitutes 16.4% of the remedies sought, and together with the 'damages and other remedy' option, amounts to 44.1% of all the Article 101 proceedings, whereas that combination of remedies only constitutes 31% of all remedies sought.[82] Accordingly, this reflects the expectation that a high percentage of Article 101 actions will be damages actions, and also when one looks at the cross-tabulation between provisions relied upon/remedies sought and the type of action, as set out in Tables 7 and 8, we also observe a high correlation between Article 101 and the damages remedy with follow-on actions.

81 With the exception of Article 102 where the figure is relatively low.

82 Note in this context there are missing data for 22 of the judgments. In Italy, damages actions were more frequent in domestic Article 101 cases, with 27 of the 42 damages actions in this context – 65.9%, whilst damages actions constituted 77.1% of all the Article 101 domestic equivalent rule cases yet only comprised 47.1% of all case-law. A similar pattern emerges in the UK, with 24 of 45 damages actions in relation to Article 101-53.3% and damages actions alone constituted 57.1% of all Article 101 cases as opposed to only 42.5% of all UK case-law.

Table 7 – Aggregate EU cases cross-tabulation provision/action

PROVISION RELIED UPON		ACTION		Total
		Follow-on	Stand-alone	
	Art. 101	42	237	279
	Art. 102	4	51	55
	Domestic Art. 101	59	222	281
	Domestic Art. 102	41	209	250
	Art. 101 and Domestic	16	111	127
	Art. 102 and Domestic	10	68	78
	Combination	13	176	189
Total		185	1074	1259

Table 8 – Aggregate EU cases cross-tabulation remedy/action

REMEDY		ACTION		Total
		Follow-on	Stand-alone	
	Damages	119	94	213
	Injunction	25	317	342
	Defence	9	300	309
	Declaration	11	117	128
	Pre-action disclosure	5	7	12
	Damages and other Remedy	7	166	173
	Other Combination	9	60	69
Total		185	1061	1246

126. The relationship between the damages remedy and follow-on actions is particularly clear in the UK, as demonstrated by Table 9.

Table 9 – UK cases cross-tabulation remedy/action

REMEDY		ACTION		Total
		Follow-on	Stand-alone	
	Damages	35	10	45
	Injunction	0	15	15
	Defence	0	27	27
	Declaration	2	3	5
	Pre-action disclosure	0	2	2
	Damages and other Remedy	2	10	12
Total		39	67	106

127. It had been assumed that virtually all follow-on actions would be damages actions but they only constitute 64.3% of all follow-on actions in the EU (excluding Germany) and 68.1% when combined with 'damages and other remedy' case-law. There are indeed 59 follow-on cases which are not in the damages, or damages and other remedy categories, and 33 of these alone are from the Netherlands, with 21 injunction cases and 8 defence cases as demonstrated by Table 10.

Table 10 – Netherlands cases cross-tabulation provision/remedy

PROVISION RELIED UPON	REMEDY						Total
	Damages	Injunction	Defence	Declaration	Damages and other Remedy	Other Combination	
Art. 101	4	20	10	1	0	6	41
Art. 102	0	6	4	2	0	2	14
Domestic Art. 101	2	75	35	8	1	8	129
Domestic Art. 102	0	28	4	0	1	4	37
Art. 101 and Domestic	1	8	7	1	0	1	18
Art. 102 and Domestic	0	3	1	1	0	2	7
Combination	1	32	14	8	0	7	62
Total	8	172	75	21	2	30	308

Section (V): Success in competition case-law

128. The aggregate EU data in relation to the 'success' of competition law rulings produces the unsurprising outcome that the vast majority of judgments, over two-thirds (67%) are unsuccessful with a combined total of 33% for successful (21.7%) and partially successful (11.3%) judgments combined.[83] It should be stressed again that settlements were excluded from

[83] These have been combined in assessing the results and it is surmised here that many rapporteurs will not have fully utilised the 'partially successful' option. See for example the data from Hungary and Portugal.
Cf. S. Van de Valle, *Private antitrust litigation in the European Union and Japan*, (Maklu, Antwerpen-Appeldoorn), 2013, noting the success rate in Japan at around 27% (successful or

the scope of the project, and accordingly only contentious cases proceed through court proceedings (at various stages), and this may at least partly explain the low success rate.

129. What is remarkable is that over a wide range of Member States,[84] the figures for unsuccessful/successful and partially successful combined are broadly similar:[85] Belgium (68.4% unsuccessful, 31.6% successful (23.1%)/ partially successful(8.5%));[86] Netherlands (72.7% unsuccessful, 27.3% successful (22.1%)/partially successful(5.2%)); Spain (73.4% unsuccessful, 26.6% successful (15.8%)/partially successful(10.8%)); and the UK (61.3% unsuccessful, 38.7% successful (27.4%)/partially successful(11.3%)).[87]

130. The French data are somewhat at odds with the general trends, and with a particularly large 'partially successful' element of 40.8% of the case-law, its combined success rate is a majority of 54.9% and a minority of cases have been unsuccessful (45.1%). There is a similar story in Italy with the case-law split evenly 50% unsuccessful and 50% successful (37.5% successful and 12.5% partially successful).[88] In the UK, the litigant relying on competition law in the dispute has been successful in a number of cases over the full period, 29 successful and 12 partially successful judgments, although the success rate is accordingly less than 40%. Over the period, there have been only 17 judgments which have been classified as substantive final judgments on the merits, and of these only 3 have been successful,[89] and one partially successful.[90]

partially successful), with 37% unsuccessful and 36% of cases settled. In particular he identified a lower success rate for injunctive relief claims than for damages actions.

84 Unfortunately there was no scope for a fuller analysis within national reports of success rates and it may be that this is one of those areas where future research may focus in identifying the rationale for any differential in the success rates across different member States. In Italy there was one notable spike in 2011 with 11 of the 17 cases being successful (10 successful and one partially successful).

85 See also Hungary and Portugal with 80% and 75% unsuccessful and 20% and 25% successful (and no partially successful case-law). With a similar level of case-law a greater success rate is evident in both Ireland and Sweden, where 54.2% and 48% of the case-law was denoted as unsuccessful and there was a combined success rate of 45.8% (29.2% successful/16.7% partially successful) and 52% (40% successful/12% partially successful) respectively. In Sweden the success rate has also been apparently increasing in recent years, notably in 2010 and 2011.

86 There was missing data for 11 cases in relation to this variable.

87 See also the State with the next highest level of case law – Austria (62.5% unsuccessful, 37.5% successful (20.3%)/partially successful (17.2%)).

88 Denmark, albeit with a very much smaller level of case-law – 10 Danish cases within the project parameters -is also an outlier, with a combined 70% in the successful categories (50% successful and 20% partially successful).

89 *EWS Ltd v E.ON UK plc* [2007] EWHC 599 (Comm); *Calor Gas Ltd v Express Fuels (Scotland) Ltd* 2008 SLT 123, and 2011 *Purple Parking Ltd v Heathrow Airport Ltd* [2011] EWHC 987 (Ch).

90 *Hendry v World Professional Billiards & Snooker Association Ltd* [2002] E.C.C. 8.

131. If one looks at the aggregated data for success cross-tabulated with other case-law variables this may provide further insights into the development of the case-law across the EU, and in specific Member States. Although there is little discussion in the national reports explaining or justifying the relative success rate,[91] the set of cross-tabulated data which may provide significant insights is the relationship between success and the type of action raised, i.e. the relative rates of success in follow-on and stand-alone actions, as set out in Table 11.

Table 11 – Aggregate EU cases cross-tabulation action /success

ACTION		SUCCESS			Total
		Successful	Partially Successful	Unsuccessful	
	Follow-on	70	35	80	185
	Stand-alone	201	106	755	1062
Total		271	141	835	1247

132. Although follow-on actions are considerably less frequent (185 follow-on actions in total compared with 1062 stand-alone cases)[92] they have a relatively much higher combined success rate at 56.8% (37.8% successful and 18.9% partially successful) than stand-alone actions which have a combined success rate at 28.9% (18.9% successful and 10% partially successful). The difference is striking – an overall success rate in follow-on actions at virtually double that of stand-alone actions. This will of course reflect the fact that in follow-on actions, normally[93] the party relying on competition law will be able to rely on the earlier infringement decision to some extent,[94] and this will facilitate their claim. Moreover, the existence of particular follow-on mechanisms and specialist tribunals/courts in some States may also help,[95] not necessarily by making it easier to succeed

91 The Austrian rapporteur noted that, to some extent, the low success rate may also relate to the fact that the Cartel Court may only adopt injunctions if the alleged anti-competitive conduct is still on-going at the time of the decision being rendered by the Cartel Court.

92 Note that the data for twenty-one cases in relation to this issue were missing.

93 Certainly when dealing with EU Commission infringement decisions as a result of Article 16 Regulation 1/2003.

94 See discussion in Chapter 2, B. Rodger (ed), *Comparative Private Enforcement and Collective Redress Across the EU* (Kluwer Law Publishing, 2014).

95 Although note the very high success rate, albeit in a very small sample of only 18 follow-on cases in Spain, with 50% successful and 16.7% partially successful, compared to a much smaller success rate of 42/305 cases (13.8%) and 32/305 (10.5%) in stand-alone cases.

with claims but by facilitating a greater awareness and understanding of the types of issue inherent in competition law claims and defences.[96] Nonetheless, despite the lower overall success rate, the data indicates that there have been over 300 successful, or partially successful, stand-alone actions across Europe during the project period, establishing competition law infringements in many cases which had not (at least previously) been uncovered by the competition authorities.

133. Noting that follow-on actions tend to be damages actions, in cross-tabulating the relationship between success and the remedy sought across the EU as set out in Table 12,[97] the only really notable point is the relatively high success for damages actions across the EU, at 45.5% combined (26.8% successful and 18.8% partially successful).

Table 12 – Aggregate EU cases cross-tabulation remedy/success

REMEDY		SUCCESS			Total
		Successful	Partially Successful	Unsuccessful	
	Damages	57	40	116	213
	Injunction	85	23	233	341
	Defence	62	25	222	309
	Declaration	31	4	93	128
	Pre-action disclosure	2	5	5	12
	Damages and other Remedy	23	28	122	173
	Other Combination	10	16	43	69
Total		270	141	834	1245

Conclusion

134. This project has demonstrated that damages actions are only a part of the story of the private enforcement of competition law rights and obligations and that other remedies are more prominent in the competition litigation practice in many Member States. Although this may cast doubt as to

96 See for instance the approach of the Irish courts in relation to ice-cream freezer exclusivity in the 1990s as discussed by B Rodger 'The Big Chill for National Courts: Reflections on Market foreclosure and Freezer Exclusivity under Art 81' (2004) 11 Irish Journal of European Law 77.

97 Note that the data for 23 cases in relation to this issue were missing.

the ubiquity of compensation as the primary objective of litigation it does not necessarily call into question the principle of promotion of damages actions by the adoption of suitable institutional mechanisms to encourage and facilitate (normally follow-on) damages actions, in particular where these can complement other forms of action and remedies to ensure competition law rights and obligations are enforced effectively. I have stressed that this project is modelled on a conception of private enforcement that is rights or justice-based as opposed to approaches concerned with efficiency and concerns with duplication of enforcement costs – although the number of successful stand-alone actions across the EU evidenced by the data is an important indicator of the detection of new violations. Of course the empirical data produced in this project is only partial, for a number of methodological reasons, but in particular the 'hidden story' of litigation settlements means that this study is addressing what may be only the 'tip of the iceberg' in terms of competition law practice. The project outcomes emphasised the potential influence of the legal framework and institutional mechanisms (and also cultural development) in relation to the range of different national narratives on the development of competition litigation practice,[98] although some general EU-wide trends also stand out such as the predominance of stand-alone B2B contractual disputes, notably in Germany, the Netherlands and Spain. Moreover, the frequency of damages actions is increasing in many Member States, with litigation pending in various contexts, and there are also some limited specific damages success stories evidenced across some of the Member States, as detailed in the national reports.

98 See in particular discussion in Chapter 2, and 9 B. Rodger (ed), *Comparative Private Enforcement and Collective Redress Across the EU* (Kluwer Law Publishing, 2014), and also Chapter 6 'Comparing Economic Incentives Across EU Member States' by M. Hviid and J. Peysner.

PART II: NATIONAL COURTS' PERSPECTIVE – BINDING EFFECT OF NCA DECISIONS

■

JACQUELINE RIFFAUT SILK*

SECTION (I): Introduction

135. What does "binding effect" stand for?

136. Even since the early seventies, the CJEU has made clear that EU competition law produces direct effects in relations between individuals and creates subjective rights that have to be safeguarded by national courts.[1] This allowed the General Court to rule that the Commission was entitled to reject a complaint for lack of sufficient Community interest, based, inter alia on the possibility for the prejudiced parties to seek relief before a national court.[2] It was not before 2001 that the CJEU ruled, in the Courage Crehan case, that private parties who have suffered a loss due to an infringement of articles 81 or 82 (now 101 or 102 TFEU) have the right to claim an appropriate compensation before the competent national court.[3]

137. As ruled in the Delimitis (C-234/89) and Masterfoods (C-344/98) decisions, uniform application of EU law requires that national courts must comply with the decisions taken by the Commission and EU courts. The ruling is clear: national courts cannot contradict the decisions taken by the Commission, as well as by EU courts were the cases brought before them.

138. As indicated in these decisions, the grounds of such an obligation are to be found in the duty of sincere cooperation between the courts, the Commission and the EU courts, and also in the need of legal

---

* Jacqueline Riffaut Silk, Judge at Cour de Cassation, France.

1 Court of Justice of the European Union (CJEU), 30 Jan 1974, case 127/73, BRT and Sabam.

2 The General Court of the European Union (GCEU), 18 Sept 1992, T-24/90, Automec v Commission, para 84 s.

3 CJEU, 20 sept 2001, C-453/99, Courage and Crehan.

certainty, effectiveness and efficiency of the implementation of EU competition law.

1. The principle of legal certainty[4]

139. *"Account should be taken of the risk of national courts taking decisions which conflict with those taken or envisaged by the Commission in the implementation of article 85(1) and 86, and also article 85(3). Such conflicting decisions would be contrary to the* ***general principle of legal certainty*** *and must, therefore, be avoided when national courts give decisions on agreements or practices which may subsequently be the subject of a decision by the Commission".*

2. The obligation of sincere cooperation between, on the one hand, national courts, and on the other, the Commission and the EU courts[5]

140. "... *It is even more important that when national courts rule on agreements or practices which are already the subject of a Commission decision they cannot take decisions running counter to that of the Commission, even if the latter's decision conflicts with a decision given by a national court of first instance (...)*

It should be borne in mind that application of the Community competition rules is based on an ***obligation of sincere cooperation*** *between the national courts, on the one hand, and the Commission and the Community Courts, on the other, in the context of which each acts on the basis of the role assigned to it by the Treaty (...)*

If a national court stays proceedings, it is incumbent on it to examine whether it is necessary to order interim measures in order to safeguard the interests of the parties pending final judgment".

141. Article 16 (1) of the Regulation 1/2003 echoes these rulings.

"*When national courts rule on agreements, decisions or practices under art. 81 or art. 82 of the Treaty (now 101 or 102 TFEU) which are already the subject of a Commission's decision, they cannot take decisions running counter to the decision adopted by the Commission. They must*

4 CJEU, 28 Feb 1991, C-234/89, Delimitis, para 47.

5 CJEU, 14 Dec 2000, C-344/98, Masterfoods, para 51 seq.

also avoid giving decisions which would conflict with a decision contemplated by the Commission in proceedings it has initiated. To that effect, the national court must assess whether it is necessary to stay its proceedings. This obligation is without prejudice to the rights and obligations under article 234 of the Treaty".

142. One may observe that the Regulation stayed "halfway", since only the decisions taken by the Commission and the EU courts are declared binding for the national courts. These provisions do not cover decisions on infringement taken by national competition authorities and courts.

3. Effectiveness and efficiency

143. The Green Paper issued on 19 December 2005, then the White Paper issued on 2 April 2008, both by the Commission, outlined the need of developing private actions throughout Europe, notably by alleviating the burden of proof of the fault which lies on the claimant.

144. It was noted that provisions similar to article 16 of the Regulation existed throughout Europe only in some Member States. As a consequence, in the others, defendants in civil procedures for damages resulting from anticompetitive practices for which they had been sanctioned, could call into question their own breach of article 81 or 82 although established in a decision of a competition authority, possibly confirmed by a review court, and the courts seized with the action for damages were required to re-examine the facts and legal issues already investigated and assessed by a specialised public authority.

145. It was observed that such duplication of factual and legal analysis resulted in considerable extra costs, duration and imponderability for the victim's action for damages, and that there was no reason why a final decision taken by a NCA on article 81 or 82 in the European Competition Network (ECN), and a final judgement by a review court upholding the NCA decision or itself finding an infringement, should not be accepted in every Member State as irrebuttable proof of the infringement in subsequent civil and antitrust damages cases.[6] Such a rule, according to the White Paper, would have increased the consistent application of articles 81 and 82 by different national bodies, also the legal certainty attached to competition

[6] White Paper, pt 2.3.

decisions, and significantly strengthened **the effectiveness and procedural efficiency** of actions for antitrust damages.[7]

146. In turn, the proposal of directive released in June 2013 addresses this issue.

147. Its article 9 provides that

"*Member States shall ensure, where national courts rule, in actions for damages under article 101 or 102 of the Treaty or under national competition law, on agreements, decisions or practices which are already the subject of a final infringement decision by a national competition authority or by a review court, those courts cannot take decisions running counter to such finding of an infringement.*

This obligation is without prejudice to the rights and obligations under article 267 of the Treaty".

148. It cannot be denied that the extension of the binding effect rule, as envisaged by the proposal of directive, constitutes an appropriate response to the uncertainties, inconsistencies and inefficiencies resulting from the variety of the national systems adopted throughout Europe in the application of EU competition law (2.2.).

149. However, its application to the three elements required in tort liability – namely fault, harm and link of causation – involves some precautions (2.3.).

150. Finally, the practicalities entailed by such a reform should not be underestimated (2.4.).

Section (II): The need for convergence

1. The scope of the Proposal

151. It appears that the scope covered by the Proposal is at the same time stricter and larger than the regime organized in article 16(1) of Regulation 1/2003. It is stricter, insofar as only a final decision on infringement, prior to the decision of the national court seized with an action for damages, is mentioned.

---

7 *Ibid.*

152. But article 9 of the Proposal is also wider in scope, as NCA decisions would be binding throughout the Community, when final, were the action for damages based on an infringement either of articles 101 and 102 of the Treaty, or national competition law.

153. On this latter point, that was not mentioned in the white Paper,[8] the explanatory memorandum of the Proposal does not give many details in the section dedicated to the probative effect of national decisions.[9]

154. Other parts of the document[10] are more explicit.

155. It is observed that the scope of the directive goes beyond giving effect only to articles 101 and 102 of the Treaty, insofar as that the proposed directive "*also modifies the applicable national rules concerning the right to claim damages for infringement of national competition law, even if that is only in respect to anticompetitive behaviour that has an effect on trade between Member States and to which EU competition law equally thus applies*", so that the proposed directive has also to be based on article 114 TFEU.[11]

156. Also, the Memorandum adds[12] that "*in cases where compensation is sought for a violation of both EU and national competition law, it is appropriate for the same substantive and procedural rules to apply to those damages actions. Applying diverging rules on civil liability for a single specific instance of anticompetitive behaviour would not only make it unworkable for judges to handle the case, it would also imply legal uncertainty for all parties involved, and it could lead to conflicting results depending on whether the national court considers the case as an infringement of EU or of national competition law, thus hampering the effective application of those rules. The proposed Directive therefore refers to damages actions for "infringements of national or EU competition law", or jointly "infringements of competition law" whereby "national competition law" is defined narrowly so as to cover only cases where it is applied in parallel to EU competition law*".

157. As recalled by the Preamble of the Proposal,[13] these provisions can be read in light of article 3 of Regulation 1/2003, which has instituted a

8 White Paper, para 2.3 p. 6.
9 Explanatory Memorandum, pt 4.3.
10 Explanatory Memorandum, Legal basis of the proposal, pt 3.1 p. 10.
11 *Ibid.*, p. 10 para 4.
12 *Ibid.*, para 4.1, Scope and definitions.
13 Preamble, recital 9.

principle of primacy of EU competition law, when the practices at stake may affect trade between Member States.[14] It is noted in the Preamble that "*applying diverging rules on civil liability for infringements of article 101 and 102 of the Treaty and for infringements of rules of national competition law which must be applied in the same case and in parallel to Union competition law would otherwise adversely affect the position of claimants in the same case and the scope of their claims, and constitute an obstacle to the proper functioning of the internal market*".

158. They might nonetheless give rise to delicate debates before the national courts seized with actions for damages, and at least significantly extend the reach of the Proposal, possibly leading to the modification of national rules regardless the affectation of EU trade, due to the need of consistency in the application of competition law whether national or European.

159. It has to be noted that article 9 of the Proposal was finally modified in a more restrictive perspective. The general approach adopted on 3 December 2013 by the Council in December 2013[15] limits the scope of the binding effect given to national decisions to the actions for damages brought before the national courts of the same Member State. Also it provides that it will be possible to present before national courts final decisions given in another Member State, "*as evidence in accordance with the national legislation, among other, of the fact that an infringement of competition law has occurred*".

2. The diversity of national rules applicable to damages actions throughout Europe

160. A large variety of regimes have been adopted in Member States.

161. Under the French regime, for example, a competition decision taken by the Competition Authority is not binding on the judge, unlike a decision

---

14 To that effect, art. 3 (1) of Regulation 1/2003 provides that "where NCAs of the Member States or national courts apply national competition law to agreements... or concerted practices within the meaning of article 81 of the Treaty which may affect trade between Member States ... they shall also apply article 81 ... Where NCAs or national courts apply national competition law to any abuse prohibited by article 82 ... they shall also apply article 82".
Similarly, art. 3 (2) provides that "the application of national competition law may not lead to the prohibition of agreements ... or concerted practices which may affect trade between Member States but which do not restrict competition within the meaning of art. 81 (1) ... or which fulfil the conditions of article 81 (3) ... or which are covered by a Regulation for the application of art. 81(3) ...".

15 Proposal of directive, general approach adopted by the Council on 3.12.2013, n ° 17317/13.

taken by the Commission. This was confirmed by the Cour de Cassation in 2001: whereas the Competition Council had sanctioned an undertaking because it had restricted the supply of a customer in an anticompetitive way, the judge dismissed the claim for damages, due to a lack of evidence of the infringement.

162. Thus, the Commercial Court ruled[16] that:

163. "It is incumbent to the one who alleges the existence of discriminatory practices to prove them; having decided, after an appreciation of the elements produced by the parties, *including the decision invoked of the Competition Council, which, contrary to the plea, is not binding for the judge*, and without altering the terms of the said decision, that the plaintiff did not establish any of the facts imputed to X..., the court of appeal has legally justified its decision".

164. However, in practice, the prior competition decision has a high probative value for the civil judge. In a more recent decision,[17] the Commercial Chamber went even further, not criticising the statement of the court of appeal that the question of abuse of dominance had been previously decided by the Competition Authority and was not to be discussed again.

165. In Italy and Spain, where principles similar to the French ones have been maintained, only the decisions taken by the Commission and the Community Courts have a binding effect on civil courts seized of damages actions in both countries.

166. On the contrary, Germany and the UK follow different rules. In Germany, a reform of the Act on Restrictions of Competition (ARC) applicable since 2005 gave binding effect to the decisions of German competition authorities and also to those of other European national competition authorities, on the civil courts as far as damages claims for antitrust violations were concerned.

167. In the UK, the Enterprise Act 2002 introduced a new procedure as an alternative to bringing a claim for damages in court, by which a person who has suffered a loss or damage as a result of the infringement of a "relevant prohibition" may make a claim before the Competition Appeal Tribunals (the CAT), which is bound by any relevant decision – taken by either the Commission and the EU courts or the UK national and sectorial regulators.

16 Com. 17 July 2001, n° 99 17251, *STEA c. Magnetti Marelli*.
17 Com. 23 March 2010, n° 08 21768, 08 20427, Bes v France Telecom and Mr Bes.

168. Decisions taken by European courts, and national ones in private actions for damages, bring some useful insight on the matter. On the legal side, and on the practical one, what can be inferred, for now, from the Proposal if the directive was to be adopted and implemented?

Section (III): The binding effect rule and the legal elements of tort liability

169. Tort liability, which applies to damages actions based on competition law infringements, requires, as a general standard in national civil law throughout the Community, the proof of three elements: fault, harm, and causation between the two.

1. The fault

170. The presumption that this requirement is satisfied, in a civil action for damages, by a former decision on the infringement, has serious consequences on the jurisdiction of the tribunal seized with the claim for damages, also on the rights of the defence granted to the defendant in the civil action. The civil judge will not have to discuss the facts and the reasoning upon which the regulator motivated its decision that there was an infringement to competition law. Likewise, the defendant in the civil action will be deprived of any possibility to discuss the Competition Authority's decision although it is the basis of the claim. It follows that such a presumption should be justified only if the defendant has had, prior to the civil action for damages, the possibility to discuss the findings of infringement, and the possibility to appeal the decision on public enforcement.

171. Two points arise here: the need of a decision identified as such, and the necessary protection of the rights of the defence.

1.1. The fault requirement: a decision

172. The civil court will have to verify whether the Authority actually "decided" that the facts which are the basis of the claim for damages, constituted an infringement.

173. As a consequence, what is needed is not only findings of facts by the Authority, but a decision of the latter qualifying the facts with regard to competition law.

174. This decision must be identified as such by the court deciding on the damages claim: the tribunal ought to reject cases where there is no clearly identifiable finding of infringement and where they are in effect being asked to make their own judgment on that issue.

175. UK jurisprudence gives an interesting illustration of this, in a case where the Court of appeal granted the defendant an authorisation to appeal a judgment of the Competition Appeal Tribunal (CAT), awarding damages to Enron Coal Services Ltd (ECSL) following a decision of the railway regulator ORR taken against English Welsh & Scottish Railway (EWS) for abuse of dominance and price discrimination.[18]

176. The Court of Appeal stated that:

> *"Court's task is not to establish liability but to deal with causation & quantum after having identified the findings of infringement. The role of the tribunal is limited to the determination of loss which results from a finding of infringement by a regulator. The tribunal is not therefore concerned with the correctness of that finding but only with whether it has been made. Any challenge to the finding of infringement has to be resolved on an appeal to the tribunal under art. 46 of CA 1998; not in proceedings under 47 A.*[19] *The tribunal is, for those purposes, bound by the finding which the regulator has made. His function is to do no more than to identify the findings of infringement in the decision (...)".*

177. The same judgment observes that "*the Tribunal's decision neatly illustrates the dangers of not taking a sufficiently strict approach as to what findings of infringement the regulator has in fact made*".[20]

178. One may note that the Competition Appeal Tribunal's rules precisely require the claimant to submit a Claim Form which contains a concise statement of the relevant facts, "*identifying any relevant findings in the decision on the basis of which the claim for damages is being made*", and also a concise statement of any contention of law relied on".[21] Moreover,

---

18 UK Court of Appeal, 1st July 2009, case n° C3/2009/0815/PTA, English Welsh & Scottish Railway ltd v Enron Coal Services ltd, para 28.

19 Section 46 CA 1998 provides that any party to an agreement in respect of which the OFT has made a decision, or any person in respect of whose conduct the OFT has made a decision, may appeal to the CAT against, or with respect to, the decision.
Section 47A CA 1998 gives a person who has suffered loss or damage by virtue of an infringement of EU or UK competition law the right to bring a monetary claim before the CAT.

20 *Ibid.*, para 59.

21 Competition Appeal Tribunal's ("CAT") Rules, rule 32(3)(a) and (b).

the Tribunal's Guide to Proceedings recommends that the parties should concisely identify the facts found in the decision that are alleged to have caused loss.[22]

179. However the "split" jurisdiction of regulator for infringement, and civil court for causation and assessment of damages may need some reconsideration, as observed by Lord Justice Jacob in this case:[23]

> "*What if, for instance, the regulator makes a clear finding of facts (e.g. about causation) which is not necessary for its determination of infringement. Would that finding arguably be outside its jurisdiction and hence not a finding which could be relied upon in a follow-on claim? In this context, it must be remembered that the party claiming damages is not a party to the proceedings before the regulator. Facts about causation and damages, which will normally include an investigation into whether and if so how the infringing conduct affected that particular party, are not necessarily a part of the regulator's inquiry. If one is not careful there could be an injustice: findings made by the regulator on incomplete evidence followed by an impossibility of attacking them later (...)*".

180. In other words, the rights of the defence might be undermined in a follow-on action for damages, if the fault requirement and the link of causation were deduced of facts that are present in the decision of the regulator, but do not constitute a finding of infringement as such.

181. This leads to a further question: will the decision on infringement be binding on a whole, only for its operative part, or is a more nuanced approach needed?

182. On this point, the General Court ruled[24] that "*the assessments made in the grounds of a decision can be subject to judicial review by the Community judicature only to the extent that, as grounds of a measure adversely affecting a person's interests, they constitute an essential basis for the operative part of that measure[25] and if, in particular, those grounds are likely to alter the substance of what was decided in the operative part of the measure in question*".[26]

---

22 CAT's Guide to Proceedings, para 6.82.
23 UK Court of Appeal, 19 January 2011, Enron v EWS, para 148 seq.
24 GCEU, T-474/04, 12 Oct 2007, Pergan, para 73.
25 GCEU, T-213/00, *CMA CGM & al c. Commission*, para 186.
26 GCEU, T-251/00, *Lagardère & Canal + c. Commission*, para 67 & 68.

183. Similarly, the French Cour de Cassation, in Plenary Session, ruled that "*res judicata applies only to what has been the matter of a judgement and was decided in its operative part*".[27]

1.2. The fault requirement: an addressee

184. The second question to be addressed by the court seized with a claim for damages is whether the defendant (in the civil action) was an addressee of the decision (in the public enforcement procedure), so that he had effectively the possibility to exercise his rights of defence.

185. In other words, was a statement of objections notified to the defendant, did he have access to the file and the effective possibility to present his defence, was he named and sanctioned in the decision so that he could appeal the decision?

186. In the case Iberian UK Ltd v BPB industries,[28] Laddie J held that:

> "*A decision of the EU Commission addressed to a particular undertaking to the effect that the undertaking has committed breaches of article 82 (now art. 102 TFUE), was binding on the undertaking, and could be relied on by third parties in national courts, so that the relevant undertaking could not deny that it had committed the infringements found by the Commission to have occurred*".

187. The point was further developed by the General Court[29] in a case where an application was made for the annulment of a Commission decision insofar as it rejected the applicant's request for the removal of all references to it in the definitive published version of the decision. Proceedings had been closed against the applicant by reason of time limits. In the operative part, the decision did not refer to the applicant's participation in the infringement found. However it stated in the grounds of the decision, in relation to the applicant, a detailed description of the applicant's participation in the main cartel.

188. The Court declared the request for annulment well founded and annulled the decision of the Commission: "*regardless of whether or not the Commission was justified in finding, in the grounds of the P...*

---

27 Ass. Plen. 13 March 2009, Bull. 3, n° 08 16033.
28 1996 2 CMLR 601.
29 GCEU, 12 Oct 2007, T-474/04, *Pergan c. Commission*.

decision, an infringement attributable to the applicant, in the absence of such a finding in the operative part, the applicant did not have standing to bring an action against that decision (which) would have been inadmissible (...)".[30]

189. The Court added that "*the presumption of innocence implies that every person accused is presumed to be innocent until his guilt has been established according to law. It thus precludes any formal finding and even any allusion to the liability of an accused person for a particular infringement in a final decision unless that person has enjoyed all the usual guarantees accorded for the exercise of the rights of the defence (...)*".

190. On this issue, the Berlin Higher Regional Court[31] held in a case where were disputed various questions concerning the private enforcement of cartel damages claims under the ARC, that there was a *prima facie* evidence that a defendant was a member of a (hard-core) cartel if he was named in the grounds of a fine decision of the Federal Cartel Office (FCO). The Court overturned the Regional Court's judgement that had dismissed the claim, and awarded compensation.

191. For deciding so, the Court observed that the defendant was one of four affiliated operative companies of a company which was one of the main members of the cartel, and that the addressee of the fine decision was the director of the defendant as well as of the other three operative companies.

192. However the defendant was not an addressee of the decision on infringement, nor did the FCO deal with the participation of the defendant in the operative part of the decision.

193. Seized with an action for damages following a decision of sanction of the Commission confirmed by the European courts,[32] the Court of Appeal of Paris had to answer a similar question relating to the probative value of elements contained in the decision, while the defendants – subsidiaries of the sanctioned company also sued by the claimant – argued that the fault requirement was not established, since no sanction had been pronounced against them. The court observed that article 16 of the Regulation was not applicable as such to them, adding that this circumstance was not an

[30] Para 74 seq.
[31] Kammegericht Berlin, 1st Oct. 2009, case n° Az. 2 U 10/03 Kart.
[32] GCEU, T-158/9913, Jan. 2004; EUCJ, C-167/04 P, 21 Sept. 2006, JBC Services.

obstacle to taking into account, in light of the evidence submitted by the parties, facts noted in the Community decisions that constituted a fault under article 1382 of the civil code.[33] These facts were not denied by the defendants.

194. Undoubtedly, "*the crucial question will lie in ascertaining the ambit of the (Competition Authority)'s decision*".[34]

2. The link of causation: effect and object

195. Public and private enforcement are different by their very nature: the first relates to the protection of markets considered as a whole, the second concerns direct relationships between undertakings and/or economic actors.

196. Hence another question arises: how to satisfy the second criterion, namely the link of causation?

197. In other words, will the causation link be inferred "automatically" from the existence of a public enforcement decision, and the assessment that the claimant was a customer of the sanctioned undertaking?

198. Or more briefly, how should the presumption work? Besides, should it be a rebuttable, or a non-rebuttable one?

199. One knows that harm must be direct, actual and certain.

200. How can the presumption apply, when the decision on infringement stated that the practices at stake had as "object" – not as "effect" – the restriction of competition?

201. The Italian Cour de Cassation answered this question,[35] quashing the judgement of a Court of appeal which considered that the harm alleged resulted "automatically" from the cartel sanctioned by the regulator. The appellants claimed that the causation link had not been demonstrated, since only the object of the sanctioned practices had been ascertained.

202. The Italian Supreme Court decided that, if the causation link may be established on the basis of presumptions and probabilities, it is incumbent

33 Court of Appeal of Paris, 26 June 2013, n° 12/04441, *société JCB Sales ltd & al. c. société Central Parts*.

34 CAT, 5 July 2012, *Travel Group Plc c. Cardiff City Transport ltd*, case n° 11/78/5/7/11, para 35.

35 Italian Cour de Cassation, 15 December 2006, *Fondiaria Societa Assicuratrice Industriale c. Nigriello*.

to the (civil) judge to take into consideration the objections opposed by the defendant and its thesis that other factors might have occurred. In other words, adds the Court, the presumption resulting from the decision on infringement is a rebuttable one, and the judge is under a duty to motivate his decision with regard to the elements produced by the defendant.

3. Existence of harm

203. Three remarks can be made.

204. Firstly, in two recent rulings,[36] the Commercial Chamber of the French Cour de Cassation excluded any presumption of causation deriving from the decision on the infringement, as well as any possibility of reversal in the burden of proof.

205. In the second case, the avocat general and the rapporteur quoted the decision of the Court of appeal, according to which "*passing on costs is the usual and normal business practice*" and concluded that the existence of harm was not proven by the claimant.

206. These decisions followed two former judgements made by the Commercial courts of Paris and Nanterre, also in the Vitamines cartel case. The actions brought by other alleged victims of members of the cartel had been similarly dismissed by reason of their failure to demonstrate that they had suffered a loss.[37]

207. In deciding so, the Cour de Cassation merely applied fundamental principles of civil law and held the plaintiff in a strict duty to discharge his burden of proof. Under French law, the latter may only obtain compensation if he proves that, in addition to being the victim of an illicit conduct, he suffered a loss that ought to be personal and direct, i.e. resulting directly from the tort, and certain. The existence of a wrongdoing does not alleviate the burden of proof.

208. It must be added that, in France, the assessment of harm, and its compensation, are a question of fact on which the Cour de Cassation has

[36] Com. 15 June 2010, n° 09 15816, *société Doux c. société Ajinomoto Eurolysine et Ceva Santé animale*; Com., 15 May 2012, n° 11 18495, *société Legouessant, société Sofral c. société Ajinomoto Eurolysine et Ceva santé animale.*

[37] Paris TCO, 27 Jan 2007, n° RG 2003/04804, *Laboratoires Juva Santé c. Hoffmann Laroche*; Nanterre TCO, 11 May 2006, n° RG 2004FO2643, *Arkopharma c. Roche and Hoffmann Laroche.*

little control, provided the principle of full compensation, and the interdiction of a lump evaluation, have been respected.

209. One may note that the French Cour de Cassation expressed the same refusal to take for granted that anticompetitive practices generate harm to the economy when it ruled on the notion of harm to the economy, which is one of the criteria enumerated by article L 464-2 of the French Commercial Code for the determination of the sanction pronounced by the Competition Authority.

210. Thus, the Court decided that "the amount of the sanction of an anti-competitive practice must be proportionate to the importance of the harm to the economy resulting from the said practice; this harm cannot be presumed".[38]

211. However the Cour de Cassation held that a qualitative assessment of harm was sufficient, and did not require a precise quantification of it.

212. On the contrary, in the neighbouring field of unfair competition, the constant position of the French courts has been that the existence and the extent of harm must be distinguished, the former being presumed since "*unfair practices necessarily generate a commercial trouble that constitutes harm, were the latter only moral*".[39]

213. At first sight, the position taken in the current Bill for the protection of consumers may be noted. A non-rebuttable presumption of fault is set up, on which collective actions created by the same Bill will be based. Additionally, a provision decides that collective actions will be allowed only following a final public enforcement decision assessing the facts, and the fault.

214. One may think that this choice was made on the observation that, at this last level of the economic chain, passing-on practices were unlikely to happen.

---

[38] Com. 7 April 2010, Bull. 70; Com. 12 July 2011, Bull. 116; Com., 30 May 2012, n° 11 22144.

[39] Com. 28 Sept 2010, n° 09 69272.

Section (IV): How to ensure the effective implementation of the new rule?

215. This fourth point will mention briefly some practicalities attached to the implementation of a binding effect rule extended to the decisions taken by the NCAs throughout the Community, also to possible sanctions were a final decision on infringement of a NCA or court in the EU to be ignored by the claimant and/or the civil court seized with a claim for damages.

216. However it must be recalled that the scope of the binding effect has been reduced in the general approach adopted by the Council on 3 December 2013.[40] As noted above, the rule would now apply only within the same Member State. Final decisions would have only probative value if presented before civil courts of another Member State, and only "in accordance with national legislation", which lessens significantly the extent of the authority attached to the decisions of sanction taken by national competition authorities throughout Europe.

1. Access to decisions on public enforcement taken by NCAs in the EU

217. Extending to all competent national courts the binding effect of any final decision taken by NCAs in Europe would have required a full and reliable access to NCA decisions – and eventually to the judgements of reviewing courts –, understanding of their content, and a legal value given to the translated version of the decisions which would have been the basis of the court's judgement on damages.

218. However a similar observation can be made, were NCA decisions presented before national courts only as evidence. They should be made accessible and understandable for any national judge seized with civil actions for damages, whatever be the language of the former and the latter ones.

219. It seems that neither a comprehensive database, nor a legally binding translation of public enforcement decisions taken by NCAs throughout Europe have so far been provided for. Both should be set up.

[40] See above, 1-1, The scope of the Proposal.

2. Should an infringement to the binding effect rule be sanctioned?

220. The ambit of the binding effect rule extended or not to all NCA decisions in the EU regardless of the Member State concerned, can be discussed with regard to the possibility for the claimant to ignore the rule, and for the judge to set it aside.

3. Would the claimant have a choice?

221. It follows from the proposal of directive that an action for damages could only be based on the prior decision on infringement if any – in the same Member State –, due to its binding effect: no further discussion would be possible, neither on the fault, nor on the findings sustaining the decision on the fault.

222. This seems to preclude any action for damages on a general basis, if taken on the same facts. Does this leave a choice to the victim of anticompetitive practices?

223. Such issues already came up in Member States where the rule already applies.

224. On this point, the UK Court of appeal ruled[41] that:

> *"The right to bring a follow-on claim before the tribunal does not affect the right of a party to bring the sort of proceedings in court that were already possible, so a party which considers itself to have been the victim of anti-competitive behaviour, and to have suffered a loss as a result, has a choice: it may bring ordinary proceedings in the High court, or, if a relevant regulator has held there to have been an infringement, it may bring proceedings in the Tribunal".*

225. Would this reasoning remain correct, if the proposal of directive – even restricted to decisions and actions within the same Member State – was to become the law?

226. There should be a possibility, at least, for the claimant to invoke and for the court to discuss facts that are distinct from the findings on which the regulator made its decision.

41 UK Court of Appeal, ECS v EWS, 19 Jan 2011, para 8.

4. Should control of the application of the binding effect rule be given to reviewing courts?

227. Being a matter of law, and with regard to public order, should the application of the rule by civil courts, seized with actions for damages, be overseen by National Courts of appeal and ultimately by National Supreme Courts, ex officio if needed?

Conclusion

228. Extending the binding effect rule would undoubtedly facilitate civil actions for damages before national courts and strengthen the application of competition law throughout Europe. However the reform implies significant changes in national legislations that touch upon national rules in civil law and civil procedure, and should not undermine the necessary protection of the rights of the defence. Finally the full success of the reform will depend on the concrete measures that will be taken, to make it possible for civil courts to have effective access and use of decisions by national authorities and courts in Europe.

II

INITIATING A CLAIM

PART I: PLURALITY IS THE KEY: COLLECTIVE REDRESS, CONSENSUAL SETTLEMENTS AND OTHER INCENTIVE DEVICES

■

Rafael Amaro*

Section (I): EU "legal tradition" and US experience

229. European Commission's position. To introduce the panel discussion, my research paper will briefly describe and discuss recent proposals on this topic, at the EU or at the national level. Unfortunately, many important issues cannot be tackled in such a short contribution.[1] Thus, it will be limited to some salient questions more specifically related to the reception or the rejection of the U.S. experience.

My starting point is the two assumptions/two premises of the European Commission that govern its proposals:

- implementing devices consistent with the Member States "legal tradition";

---

* Rafael Amaro, Lecturer (maître de conférences) at Université Paris Descartes – Sorbonne Paris Cité.

1 See e. g. for an overview of the question: J. Basedow, *Private Enforcement of EC Competition Law*, Kluwer Law, 2007; J. Basedow, S. Francq, L. Idot (ed.), *International Antitrust Litigation: Conflict of Laws and Coordination*, Hart Publishing, 2012; J. Basedow, J. P. Terhechte, L. Tichy (ed.), *Private Enforcement of Competition Law*, Nomos, 2011; A. A. Foer, J. W. Cuneo, *The International Handbook on Private Enforcement of Competition Law*, Edward Elgar, 2010C.-D. Ehlermann, I. Atanasiu (ed.), *European Competition Law Annual 2001: Effective Private Enforcement of EC Antitrust Law*, Oxford, Hart Publishing, 2003; A. P. Komninos, *EC Private Antitrust Enforcement: Decentralised Application of EC Competition Law by National Courts*, Hart Publishing, Oxford/Portland, 2008; B. J. Rodger (ed.), *Comparative Private Enforcement & Consumer Redress in the EU*, study for the *Arts & Humanities Research Council*, available at: http://www.clcpecreu.co.uk/default.htm. See e. g. *in* French: M. Dumarçay, *La situation de l'entreprise victime dans les procédures de sanction des pratiques anticoncurrentielles*, préf. B. Lasserre, Litec, 2010; S. Pietrini, *L'action collective en droit des pratiques anticoncurrentielles*, Bruylant, 2012; R. Amaro, *Le contentieux privé des pratiques anticoncurrentielles. Etude des contentieux autonome et complémentaire devant les juridictions judiciaires*, Bruylant, 2013.

- restricting the number of devices as a consequence of this attention brought to the "legal tradition".[2]

230. "American product export." I believe that the "legal tradition" argument is overrated. It is mainly put forward to dismiss devices inspired by the U.S. model of private antitrust litigation[3]. This leads the European Commission in its June 11th 2013 "package" (*i.e.* the proposal for a directive on actions for damages and in its recommendation for collective redress) to exclude some "U.S. devices" such as the opt-out class actions[4] or the contingency fees.

The private enforcement of competition law is an *"American product export"*:[5] my opinion is that the 100 years of U.S. experience cannot just be ignored when addressing the crucial question of its spreading across Europe.

231. Lande-Davis study. Some statistics of the Lande-Davis study clearly highlight the attractive features of the U.S. devices.[6] This study evaluates 40 of the largest U.S. private antitrust cases between 1990 and 2007 for a cumulative recovery of 18 to 19.6 billion U.S. dollars. Of this amount:

- 42 to 46% (7.6 to 8.9 billion) came from stand-alone litigation and only a third came from follow-on litigation (the rest was mixed between public and private origin).
- 34/40 cases were class actions, mostly opt-out class actions.

---

2 The position of the European Commission is clear: *"(15) Collective redress mechanisms should preserve procedural safeguards and guarantees of parties to civil actions. In order to avoid the development of an abusive litigation culture in mass harm situations, the national collective redress mechanisms should contain the fundamental safeguards identified in this Recommendation. Elements such as punitive damages, intrusive pre-trial discovery procedures and jury awards, most of which are foreign to the legal traditions of most Member States, should be avoided as a general rule." Recommendation of 11 June 2013 on common principles for injunctive and compensatory collective redress mechanisms in the Member States concerning violations of rights granted under Union Law, Official Journal*, L 201, 26/07/2013, pp. 60 – 65.

3 H.-W. Micklitz, "Collective Private Enforcement in Antitrust Law – What is Going Wrong in the Debate", *in* J. Basedow, J. P. Terhechte, L. Tichy (ed.), *Private Enforcement of Competition Law*, Nomos, 2011, p. 101 *sqq.*, at pp. 114 to 117.

4 J. G. Delatre, "Beyond the White Paper: Rethinking the Commission's Proposal on Private Antitrust Litigation", *Comp. L. Rev.*, 2011, vol. 8(1), p. 29 *sqq.*, at pp. 31 et 32.

5 J. W. Cuneo, "Differing traditions", *in* A. A. Foer, J. W. Cuneo (dir.), *The International Handbook on Private Enforcement of Competition Law*, Edward Elgar, 2010, p. 27 *sqq.*, at p. 32.

6 R. H. Lande, J. P. Davis, "Benefits From Private Antitrust Enforcement: An Analysis of Forty Cases", *USF L. Rev.*, 2008, vol. 42, p. 882 *sq*, updated in R. H. Lande, "Benefits of private enforcement: empirical background", *in* A. A. Foer, J. W. Cuneo (dir.), *The International Handbook on Private Enforcement of Competition Law*, Edward Elgar, 2010, p. 3 *sq*, at pp. 5 to 7.

232. These astonishing statistics for European observers call to mind the limits of European legal framework. That is probably one of the reason why Lord Denning, in his inimitable style, wrote thirty years ago:

> *"As a moth is drawn to the light, so is a litigant drawn to the United States. If he can only get his case into their courts, he stands to win a fortune. At no cost to himself, and at no risk of having to pay anything to the other side."*[7]

233. Recently, the evolutions of the U.S. Supreme court case law tend to limit forum and law shopping, making more difficult for the plaintiffs to sue the defendants in U.S. courts. As a matter of fact, Lord Denning's observation is not as true as what it was once. Reforming European law is thus an urgent challenge in order to provide efficient rules to European plaintiffs. But how?

234. A wide-ranging litigation. Private antitrust litigation is manifold. It can involve local or international scale damages. It can harm consumers or businesses, direct purchasers or indirect purchasers, one supplier or millions of buyers. It can result from EU wide cartels or local abuses of dominance. It can follow public enforcement or not.

235. My point is that this wide-ranging litigation can only be tackled by a wide range of rules. In this respect, the cultural diversity of rules originating from the U.S. and rules originating – or allegedly originating – from Europe (*e.g.* opt-in group action, follow-on litigation and other kinds of incentive devices like public funding) is a great opportunity.

236. There is no need to choose only one device: plurality is the key.

237. Scope of the paper. The first section of this paper deals with collective redress mechanisms. Two kinds of collective redress which exist in EU Member States law will be discussed:

- group actions where a category of victims brings legal actions to enforce collective claims seeking the compensation of individual damages (such as the U.S. class action). In group actions, the trial is carried out by a victim, an *ad hoc* person, a consumer association or a public authority on behalf of the relevant group of persons. The judgment will bind all the persons represented by the acting party, *i.e.* the persons who opted in or opted out depending on the system of representation adopted. It means that in group actions, represented individuals are parties to the proceedings.

[7] *Smith Kline and French Laboratories, Ltd., et al. v. Bloch* [1983] 2 All E.R. 72, 74 (C.A.1982).

- representative collective actions where an organization, a public authority or an individual bring legal action on behalf of a group of victims, who are not parties to the proceedings.

238. The second section of this paper deals with consensual settlements, *i.e.* out-of-court dispute resolution settled by a contract between the claimants and the defendants.

239. In the third section dedicated to the incentive devices, I will focus on the ways to encourage private and public funding of the private enforcement.

Section (II): Collective redress: Opt-in? Opt-out? Both? / Follow-on? Stand alone? Both? / Group actions? Representative actions? Both?

1. Do opt-in systems work?

240. Mulheron and Leuven studies. Opt-in or opt-out? This is a recurring debate now that there is a quasi-consensus on the opportunity of group actions[8] and its supplemental contribution to deter infringements.[9]

---

8 See on this "quasi-consensus" among many references: J. Almunia, "Common standards for group claims across the EU", speech of oct. 15th 2010, Valladolid, SPEECH/10/554; D. Demougin, "Class Action from an Economic Point of View", *in* D. Cohen (ed.), *Droit et économie du procès civil*, LGDJ, « Droit et économie », 2010, p. 81 *sqq.*; R. P. McAfee, H. M. Mialon, S. H. Mialon, "Private v. Public Antitrust Enforcement: A Strategic Analysis", available at: http://papers.ssrn.com/sol3/papers.cfm?abstract_id=775245, 2008, p. 2; R. Posner, *Antitrust Law: An Economic Perspective*, University of Chicago Press, 1976, p. 227 *sqq.*; J. Rüggeberg, M. P. Schinkel, "Consolidating Antitrust Damages in Europe: A Proposal for Standing in line with Efficient Private Enforcement", Amsterdam Center for Law & Economics, Working Paper No. 2006-04, available at: http://ssrn.com/paper=903282; R. Van den Bergh, L. Visscher, "The Preventive Function of Collective Actions for Damages in Consumer Law", *Erasmus Law Review*, 2008, vol. 1, p. 5; W. Wils, *The Optimal Enforcement of EC Antitrust Law. Essays in Law and Economics, Kluwer Law International*, 2001, p. 19 *sqq.* In French: F. Caballero, « Plaidons par procureur ! De l'archaïsme procédural à l'action de groupe », *RTD civ.*, 1985, p. 247 *sqq.*; B. Deffains (B.), « Les effets bénéfiques des actions de groupe : une approche économique », *in Vers une action de groupe… à la française, Concurrences*, n° 2-2008, p. 34 et s.; L. Rozon, « Le recours collectif favorise l'accès à la justice pour les consommateurs », *Rev. de droit de l'Université de Sherbrooke*, vol. 29, 1998-1999, p. 57 *sqq.* See also many French official reports: L. Béteille, *Rapport fait au nom de la commission des lois sur la proposition de loi sur le recours collectif*, rapp. n° 532, 2010; L. Béteille, R. Yung, *Rapport d'information fait au nom de la commission des lois par le groupe de travail sur l'action de groupe*, rapp. n° 499, disp. en mai 2010; G. Cerutti, M. Guillaume, *Rapport sur l'action de groupe*, 2005; J.-J. Hyest, *Rapport d'information sur les « class actions »*, rapp. n° 249, 2006; J. Attali, *Commission pour la libération de la croissance française*, 2008. Reports available on the French Senate website or on La Documentation française website.

9 P. Collins, "Public and private enforcement challenges and opportunities", Speech to the Law Society's European Group, 2006, available at: http://www.oft.gov.uk/news-and-updates/

Yet in its recent *Impact Assessment Report* accompanying the June 11th 2013 proposal, the Commission makes a stand: it dismisses the opt-out group action like it has already done in its 2008 White Paper.[10] This suspicion for the US-style system is questionable. Mr Gaudet noticed that it was not even supported by empirical evidence.[11]

241. It is true that in a study for the Civil Council Justice[12] – ignored by the Commission – Professor Mulheron found out that the participation rate for opt-out group actions was by far higher than the opt-in one (see *infra* table A). It is obvious for mass claims[13] and these 5 years-old statistics have not been invalidated by recent studies. Despite the fact that many E.U. Member States implemented opt-in group actions in the last ten years, no sudden rises of actions for damages have been observed. We can conclude that no significant evolution reversed the Mulheron study skepticism for the opt-in system.

Table 13 – Rachael Mulheron Study

TABLE 18 Rates of participation for opt-out regimes	
Jurisdiction from which empirical studies/cases emanated	**Rate of participation in the litigation ...**
Victoria	approx. 87%
United States	approx. 99.8%
Canada	approx. 60%—100%
Australia	approx. 59%-98%
Portugal	almost 100%
Netherlands	approx. 97%

speeches/2006/0306; F. Denozza, L. Toffoletti, "Compensation function and deterrence effects of private actions for damages: The case of antitrust damage suits", 2008, available at: http://papers.ssrn.com/sol3/papers.cfm?abstract_id=1116324

10 *Commission Staff Working Document: Impact Assessment Report. Damages actions for breach of the EU antitrust rules*, SWD(2013) 203 final, points 80, 82 et 195.

11 R. Gaudet, "Turning a Blind Eye: The Commission's Rejection of Opt-Out Class Actions Overlooks Swedish, Norwegian, Danish and Dutch Experience", *ECLR*, 2009, 30(3), pp. 114 et s.

12 R. Mulheron, *Reform of Collective Redress in England and Wales, A Perspective of Need*, 2008, p. 147 *sqq.* available at: http://www.judiciary.gov.uk/JCO%2FDocuments%2FCJC%2FPublications%2FOther+papers%2Freform-of-collective-redress.pdf

13 OFT, *Response to the European Commission's White Paper, Damages actions for breach of the EC antitrust rules*, 2008, points 2.3, available at: http://ec.europa.eu/competition/antitrust/actionsdamages/white_paper_comments/oft_en.pdf
We may also refer to a survey made by the CSA (a French administrative agency) at the request of two leading consumer associations in march 2007. It finds out that 77% of respondents believe consumers harmed by low-value damages will not sue in individual litigation while 83% indicate that they would seek to obtain compensation in the case of a collective judgment about them, see: R.-C. Mader-Saussaye, « Pour l'effectivité des droits des consommateurs », *in Vers une action de groupe... à la française, Concurrences*, n° 2-2008, p. 31 *sqq.*, at p. 33, footnote 39.

TABLE 19 Opt-in rates	
Jurisdiction from which empirical studies/cases emanated	Rate of participation in the litigation ...
England	approx. 0.8%-100%
United States	approx. 27%—61 %
Europe	less than 0.03%

R. Mulheron, *Reform of Collective Redress in England and Wales, A Perspective of Need*, 2008, pp. 153 and 156.

242. Opt-in systems' drawbacks. Some also argue that the opt-in system may duplicate proceedings for a single case and creates untoward risks of inconsistency.[14]

243. A worrying trend has also been pointed out in the U.S.: the opt-in model would first deter socially disadvantaged groups to sue. These groups may have a restricted access to the relevant information and even when duly informed they may experience a social or psychological inhibition and not opt in.[15] The Leuven study confirms these concerns: "*Negative elements include that the need to opt-in can be a barrier to participate in the litigation, for there may be cogent economic, psychological or social barriers preventing affirmative action being taken to opt-in.*"[16]

244. So the question can be asked in these basic terms: do we really want a legal system where only upper classes can get compensation for their unfair losses? The Commission's support for opt-in model does not address this issue.

---

14 American Bar Association, *Joint Comments on the Commission of The European Communities' White Paper on Damages Actions for Breach of the EC Antitrust Rules*, juin 2008, p. 27, available at: http://ec.europa.eu/competition/antitrust/actionsdamages/white_paper_comments/aba_en.pdf; A. Andreangelli, "Collective Redress in EU Competition Law: An Open Question with Many Possible Solutions", *World comp.*, 2012/3, p. 529 *sqq.*, at pp. 552 – 555.

15 D. Cohen, « Introduire des actions de groupe en droit français. Réactions à l'analyse du Pr. Demougin », *in* D. Cohen (ed.), *Droit et économie du procès civil*, L.G.D.J., « Droit et économie », 2010, p. 105 *sq*, at p. 110.

16 Study Centre for Consumer Law, Centre for European Economic Law (Katholieke Universiteit Leuven), *An analysis and evaluation of alternative means of consumer redress other than redress through ordinary judicial proceedings: Final Report*, Study for the European Commission, Health and Consumer Protection DG, 2007, p. 289, available at: http://www.eurofinas.org/uploads/documents/policies/OTHER%20POLICY%20ISSUES/comparative_report_en.pdf

245. In a more general perspective, the underdeterrent effect of opt-in systems may not create efficient incentives for the defendants to settle. As Mr Sorkin remarkably summed up:

> *"Global settlements are also not likely to occur in the absence of an effective collective redress mechanism. Without such a mechanism, which has the effect of aggregating individual claims and increasing a defendant's potential exposure dramatically, defendants have little incentive to settle outside the US. [...] Out-of-court settlements can only really work if they are coupled with a realistic chance of effective court action. The threat must be real if we are to achieve fair settlements. [...] the fact remains that the opt-out class action [...] is a necessary condition for any settlements where the defendants faces massive exposure from the aggregation of individual claims, because without the assurance that absent class members will be bound by settlement, no defendant will have the incentive to enter into such a settlement."*[17]

246. This statement is completely convincing. It puts into light the contradiction between two widespread positions in Europe:

- supporting opt-in-style collective redress in one hand,
- encouraging consensual settlements on the other hand (see below point 3.1).

247. If E.U. Member States really want to encourage settlements, opt-out group actions seem to be a needed prerequisite.

248. Opt-out system's benefits. In the light of the U.S. experience, some authors see the opt-out group action as a means to ensure a broader compensation, while generating high incentives for lawyers. As risk takers, lawyers will be partially paid on a percentage of the amount granted by the court (the contingency fees system). Their perspectives of gains will necessarily be more engaging in an opt-out model where the number of victims represented is structurally higher[18] which will benefit the global efficiency of private enforcement.[19]

---

17 L. T. Sorkin, "International settlements", *in* A. A. Foer, J. W. Cuneo (ed.), *The International Handbook on Private Enforcement of Competition Law*, Edward Elgar, 2010, p. 575 *sqq.*, at pp. 582 and 583.

18 T. L. Russell, "Exporting Class Actions to the European Union", *Boston U. Int. L. J.*, vol. 28, 2010, p. 141 *sqq.*, at p. 177.

19 K. C. Wildfang, S. P. Slaughter, "Funding litigation", *in* A. A. Foer, J. W. Cuneo (ed.), *The International Handbook on Private Enforcement of Competition Law*, Edward Elgar, 2010, p. 220 *sqq.*, at p. 239.

249. I do not deny the fact that the opt-out system may have drawbacks. But far from the usual caricatures, it has real qualities without falling into the excesses often highlighted. As Robert Lande states:

> *"the widespread criticisms [against the U.S. system] have been made without empirical basis. Those who point to the alleged flaws of the United States system of private antitrust enforcement support their argument only with anecdotes, many of which are self-serving or questionable. I have never seen these arguments supported with reliable data."*[20]

250. My opinion is that the strong advantages of the opt-out system for mass litigation cannot be ignored.[21] Since the aim of EU governments is to enhance the deterrent effect of private actions and to ensure the cessation of unlawful conducts, the opt-out model seems much more fitted.[22] Therefore, it is not surprising that EU Members States have adopted the opt-out system or are leaning towards systems of opt-out representation (Portugal, Denmark, Norway, Netherlands) while others intended or intend to adopt it (France[23] and U.K.[24]).

251. Mixing opt-in and opt-out. But maybe the opt-in could still fit to businesses litigation involving, for instance, SME's and large firms. If a SME wants to maintain a good relationship with a major furnisher or a major retailer, it could be more rational to avoid a litigation that will definitely damage its commercial cooperation. In this respect, it could be opportune to adopt a dual system mixing opt-out and opt-in. This combined mechanism has already been adopted in Denmark[25] and

---

20 R. H. Lande, *op. cit.*, p. 4.

21 J. Sorabji, M. Napier, R. Musgrove (ed.), *"Improving Access to Justice through Collective Actions" Developing a More Efficient and Effective Procedure for Collective Actions*, juill. 2008.

22 C. A. Jones, "Opting-in to opting-out: Why collective redress should adopt the opt-out approach to class actions", *Concurrences*, n° 2-2012 (on ligne).

23 In a rejected project of *Loi Chatel* of 2006.

24 In the Dept. for Business Innovation & Skills report of 2013: *Private actions in competition law*, point 5.16.

25 §245 e), section 9 of chapter 23 on group actions (*Gruppesøgsmål*) of the Danish Administration of Justice Act (*Lov om Rettens Pleje – Retsplejeloven*) states that opt-out representation can be ordered by a court if two conditions are met: "*1. The case must concern claims that are so small that it is evident that they cannot generally be expected to be brought in individual actions, because the inconvenience and financial risk of individual litigation are deemed to be disproportionate to the outcome of the individual action. Whether this Evaluation of the effectiveness and efficiency of collective redress mechanisms in the European Union 5 condition is satisfied will depend on the size of t he individual claims, in particular. According to the preparatory works of t he Act, this condition will normally be satisfied only if the individual claim does not exceed an amount of approximately DKK 2,000 (264 Euro). 2. A group action based on the opt-in model must be considered to be an*

Norway[26] and has been proposed in the U.K.[27] and in France.[28] It could then be up to the judge to choose the most appropriate system considering the type of damages and the number of victims.[29] For example, while for serial low-value damages, opt-out will probably be more appropriate, for damages of higher value but with fewer harmed victims, it will be the opt-in.

2. *Should group actions be limited to follow-on litigation?*

252. European Commission's position. The European Commission in its June 11th 2013 recommendations expressed a cautious position with regard to the interaction between private and public enforcement of E.U. law:

> *"In fields of law where a public authority is empowered to adopt a decision finding that there has been a violation of Union law, it is important to ensure consistency between the final decision concerning that violation and the outcome of the collective redress action. Moreover, in the case of collective actions following a decision by a public authority (follow-on actions), the public interest and the need to avoid abuse can be presumed to have been taken into account already by the public authority as regards the finding of a violation of Union law."*

---

inexpedient way of dealing with the claims, i.e. in particular if the case includes a very large number of persons so that the administration of opt-in notices will require disproportionate resources." (English translation from P. Møgelvang-Hansen, "Evaluation of the effectiveness and efficiency of collective redress mechanisms in the European Union – Country Report Denmark", 2008, pp. 4 to 5, available at: http://ec.europa.eu/consumers/redress_cons/da-country-report-final.pdf).

26 Section 35-7 of the Norwegian Dispute Act of 2005 (Lov 2005-06-17 n° 90: *Lov om mekling og rettergang i sivile tvister*) states that: *"Class actions that do not require registration of class members (1) The court can decide that persons who have claims within the scope of the class action shall be class members without registration on the class register, if the claims a) on their own involve amounts or interests that are so small that it must be assumed that a considerable majority of them would not be brought as individual actions, and b) are not deemed to raise issues that need to be heard individually."*

27 J. Sorabji, M. Napier, R. Musgrove (ed.), *op. cit.*, recommendation 3; Dept. for Business Innovation & Skills report of 2013, *op. cit., loc. cit.*

28 In the rejected project of *Loi Chatel* of 2006.

29 T. Chieu, "Class Actions In The European Union?: Importing Lessons Learned From The United States' Experience Into European Community Competition Law", *Cardozo J. International and Comparative Law*, 2010, vol. 18, p. 123 *sqq.*, at p. 154; M.-J. Azar-Baud, « L'entrée triomphale (?) de l'action de groupe en droit français », *Recueil Dalloz*, 2013, p. 1487 *sqq.*

253. Two points are important here:

- The European Commission does not exclude private stand-alone litigation.[30]
- In case of follow-on actions, the European Commission consider that no punitive sanction should be pronounced (i.e. no punitive damages or civil fine).

254. The French government's position. Both conclusions are convincing but in France, this cautious position has led to an excessive proposition. In the May 2013 *Loi Hamon* project, the French government proposed to allow only follow-on group actions and to prohibit stand-alone group actions. According to the future article L. 423-11 of the Consumer Code, the victims could only seek compensation within a five years delay after the French Competition Authority's decision that found an infringement is final (which means the defendant has exhausted all appeal avenues).

255. Stand-alone litigations' benefits. This position is not convincing. It reflects the fact that since the Green Paper of the European Commission, the private enforcement of competition law is viewed – at least in France – as only a mass consumer litigation. But consumer litigation is very unusual. Nowadays, private enforcement in Europe involves almost only businesses.[31] And in this field of private litigation: stand-alone litigation is the rule, follow-on litigation the exception (see *infra* table B and C).[32]

256. I admit that for mass consumer litigation, the economic complexity of the cases and the restricted access to evidence will certainly require prior public proceedings. But the situation is quite different for serial litigation involving businesses, like vertical contractual disputes. And it is not even sure that stand-alone group action in mass consumer litigation could not work in the future. The Lande-Davis study finds impressive data

---

30 See also its *Staff Working Document* accompanying the proposal for a directive on Damages actions, *op. cit.*, point 204.

31 C. Momège, L. Idot, "Application of Articles 81 & 82 EC by the French Ordinary Courts. A Procedural Perspective", *in* C.-D. Ehlermann, I. Atanasiu (ed.), *European Competition Law Annual 2001: Effective Private Enforcement of EC Antitrust Law*, Oxford, Hart Publishing, 2003, p. 230 *sqq.*

32 See also: S. Peyer, "Private antitrust litigation in Germany from 2005 to 2007: empirical evidence", juin 2012, *J. Competition L. & Econ*, p. 331 *sqq.*, at pp. 337 to 339; "Myths and Untold Stories – Private Antitrust Enforcement in Germany", Centre for Competition Policy Working Paper n° 10-12, 2010, available on the SSRN: http://ssrn.com/abstract=1672695; B. J. Rodger, "Competition law litigation in the UK courts: a study of all cases 2005-2008: Part 1", *GCLR*, 2009, 2(2), p. 93 *sqq.*; "Part 2", *GCLR*, 2009, 2(3), p. 136 *sqq.*

that demonstrates the efficiency of stand-alone class action in both business litigation and consumer litigation (see *infra* table D).

257. Moreover the future article L. 423-11 is not in line with article 16 § 1 of Regulation No 1/2003. This article states that in case of parallel European Commission / national courts trials, the latter are not required to stay the proceedings if it is certain that their decision will not be contrary to the Commission's. Indeed, when the national judge has no doubt about the outcome of a case in which the victims present overwhelming evidence, I do not see why it would be necessary to await a final decision of the E.U. or national competition authorities.

258. It can also be pointed out that public enforcement is long. The infringement punished by the competition authorities can be already prescribed in its civil aspects when the defendant has exhausted all appeal avenues. In addition, it is dubious that ten or fifteen years after the infringement has ceased, any victims will still be able to present material evidence.

259. Mixing follow-on and stand-alone litigation. That is why prohibiting stand-alone litigation is not consistent with the reality of European private enforcement. It should be then much more efficient to develop both models of litigation:

- follow-on actions for the most complex cases and/or for the infringements causing serial low-value damages to consumers;
- stand-alone actions for the simplest cases and/or for the infringements harming businesses (like vertical contractual disputes).

Table 14 – Private enforcement in French civil and commercial courts

	Total amount of French judgments	Litigation involving only businesses	Litigation involving not only businesses (consumer, association...)	Success rate (full or partial)	Success rate of actions for nullity	Success rate of actions for damages
Stand-alone litigation	139	133	6	39/117	17/56	15/59
Follow-on litigation	25	24	1	8/22	1/3	5/19
Total	164	157	7	47/139	18/59	20/78

Table 15 – Private enforcement in French civil and commercial courts (%)

	Total amount of French judgments	Litigation involving only businesses	Litigation involving not only businesses (consumer, association...)	Success rate (full or partial)	Success rate of actions for nullity	Success rate of actions for damages
Stand-alone litigation	84,8%	95,7%	4,3%	33,3%	30,4%	25,4%
Follow-on litigation	15,2%	96%	4%	36,4%	33,3%	26,3%
Total	100%	95,7%	4,3%	33,8%	30,5%	25,6%

R. Amaro, *Le contentieux privé des pratiques anticoncurrentielles. Etude des contentieux autonome et complémentaire devant les juridictions judiciaires*, Bruylant, (nov. 2013).

Table 16 – Lande-Davis Study

Table 3: Private Litigation Not Preceded by Government Action	
Case	*Recovery ($ millions)*
Augmentin	91
Buspirone	220
Cardizem	1 10
Taxol	66
Caldera	275
Commercial Explosives	77
Conwood	1,050
Microcrystalline Cellulose	50
NCAA	74
NASDAQ	1,027
Lease Oil	193
Paxil	165
Relafen	250
Remeron	75
Vitamins	3,908 to 5,258
Total	7,631 to 8,981

R. H. Lande, J. P. Davis, "Benefits From Private Antitrust Enforcement: An Analysis of Forty Cases", *USF L. Rev.*, 2008, vol. 42, p. 882 *sq*.

3. Are representative actions a good alternative to group actions?

260. Benefits and costs. Representative actions could embody a *"remedial scheme"* to the absence of US-style class actions.[33] They could also be an alternative pattern chosen by E.U. Member States to avoid frivolous suits that are often denounced as the excesses of the U.S. model. The representative party would indeed act as a "gate-keeper".[34] According to the Renda Study, representative actions also grant better information; significantly increase in likelihood of claim being brought, increase the expected sanction and the number of compensated victims.

But representative actions have costs. The legal proceeding could be *"slightly more costly"*, the principal-agent problems may be more accurate and the costs of distributing damages, authorization requirements, notification and opt-in (or even opt-out) could condemn this device.[35] Maybe we should not expect too much from the representative actions.

261. The French *"action en representation conjointe"*. The French experience *"action en representation conjointe"*[36] dramatically illustrates the limits of opt-in representative actions. Even if it is *strico sensu* a group action (the represented consumers are parties to the proceedings), its limits apply to opt-in representative actions. After the so-called *"cartel de la téléphonie mobile"* (one of the most serious cartel case ever judged in France), the fine imposed by the French NCA to the three mobile phone firms (Orange, SFR and Bouygues) reached 534 million euros. The leading consumer association UFC Que Choisir estimated the damage suffered by their 20 million subscribers in an amount between 1.2 and 1.6 billion euros.

---

33 E. D. Cavanagh, "The Private Antitrust Remedy: Lessons From the American Experience", *Loyola U. Chicago Law J.*, 2010, vol. 41, p. 629 *sqq.*, at p. 647.

34 D. Fairgrieve, G. Howells, "Collective Redress Procedures – European Debates", *ICLQ*, 2009, vol. 58(2), p. 379 *sqq.*, at p. 400; J. G. Delatre, *op. cit.*, p. 43.

35 A. Renda (ed.), J. Peysner, A. J. Riley, B. J. Rodger, *Making antitrust damages actions more effective in the EU: welfare impact and potential scenarios*, Report for the European Commission, 2007, pp. 341 and 342, available at: http://ec.europa.eu/competition/antitrust/actionsdamages/files_white_paper/impact_study.pdf

36 Article L. 422-1 of the French consumer code: « *Lorsque plusieurs consommateurs, personnes physiques, identifiés ont subi des préjudices individuels qui ont été causés par le fait d'un même professionnel, et qui ont une origine commune, toute association agréée et reconnue représentative sur le plan national en application des dispositions du titre Ier peut, si elle a été mandatée par au moins deux des consommateurs concernés, agir en réparation devant toute juridiction au nom de ces consommateurs. Le mandat ne peut être sollicité par voie d'appel public télévisé ou radiophonique, ni par voie d'affichage, de tract ou de lettre personnalisée. Il doit être donné par écrit par chaque consommateur.* »

The association tried then to bring an *"action en representation conjointe"* to obtain compensation for these damages. It only got 12,500 *"mandats"* (*i.e.* legal authorisation to represent the victims in court) on 20 million subscribers, representing 0.06% of the cartel's victims. Moreover, its action was eventually ruled illegal by the French Supreme Court because of the public solicitation that the association had done to inform the subscribers of the trial. So actually nobody got any compensation for the huge loss suffered...

262. Indeed, obtaining a mandate requires pretty much the same material acts as opting in for a group action. The French example highlights one fact: for serial low-value damages, victims will not opt in.

263. Mixing group actions and representative actions? Ultimately, if the representative action is to be developed in Europe, the same observations as the ones stated before for group actions would apply (see *supra* §§ 6 to 9). A combination of opt-in and opt-out mechanisms could then be appropriate. Representative actions could be necessary if the group action system does not allow public ombudsman or private association to represent the group. Otherwise it will not be necessary because the group actions initiated by such a representative actor will cover the pattern of representative action.

Section (III): Consensual settlements: Business litigation? Consumer litigation? Both? /Opt-in? Opt-out? Both?

1. Is there a need to protect settling infringers sued in further courts' litigation?

264. European Commission's position. In the U.S., more than 95% of class actions ended by a settlement.[37] Thus, the major role played by this alternative way of solving competition disputes must be taken into account.

265. It is probably one of the reason why in its recitals (37) of the June 11th 2013 directive proposal, the European Commission clearly expresses its will to encourage consensual settlements:

> *"Injured parties and infringers should be encouraged to agree on compensating the harm caused by a competition law infringement*

[37] T. Eisenberg, G. P. Miller, "Attorney Fees in Class Actions Settlements: an Empirical Study", *J. of Empirical Legal Studies*, 2004, vol. 1(1), p. 27 *sqq*.

through consensual dispute resolution mechanisms, such as out-of-court settlements, (including those where a judge can declare a settlement binding), arbitration, and mediation or conciliation. Where possible, such consensual dispute resolution should cover as many injured parties and infringers as possible. The provisions in this Directive on consensual dispute resolution are therefore meant to facilitate the use of such mechanisms and increase their effectiveness."

266. In its recital (40), the Commission makes a useful statement by insisting on the need to find consistent articulation between consensual settlements and further courts' litigation:

> "To encourage consensual settlements, an infringer that pays damages through consensual dispute resolution should not be placed in a worse position vis-à-vis its coinfringers than it would be in without the consensual settlement. This might happen if a settling infringer, even after a consensual settlement, continued to be fully jointly and severally liable for the harm caused by the infringement. A settling infringer should in principle therefore not contribute to his non-settling co-infringers when the latter have paid damages to the injured party with whom the first infringer had previously settled. The correlate to this non-contribution rule is that the claim of the injured party is reduced by the settling infringer's share of the harm caused to him, *regardless of whether the amount of the settlement equals or is different from the relative share of the harm that the settling co-infringer inflicted upon the settling injured party.* This share should be determined in accordance with the same rules used to determine the contributions among infringers (recital (27) above). Without such reduction, the non-settling infringers would be unduly affected by the settlement to which they were not a party. The settling co-infringer will still have to pay damages where that is the only possibility for the settling injured party to obtain *compensation for the remaining claim, that is the claim of the settling injured party reduced by the settling co-infringer's share of the harm that the infringement inflicted upon the settling injured party."*[38]

[38] Recitals amended by the Council of the European Union of October 24th 2013: http://register.consilium.europa.eu/pdf/en/13/st09/st09671.en13.pdf (N.B.: the excerpts in italic characters have been added by the Council. Therefore they are not in the version released in June 2013).

267. The Commission then proposed two articles to rule the interactions between settlements and courts' litigation. Article 17 of the proposal recognises the "suspensive effect of consensual dispute resolution" while article 18 deals with the "effect of consensual settlements on subsequent actions for damages". The § 1 of article 18 aims to ensure that the objective outlined in recital (40) is fulfilled. It provides three special rules:

- The first rule limits the compensation for settling victims by reducing its claim by the settling co-infringer's share of the harm that the infringement inflicted upon the injured party.
- The second rule excludes the contribution from settling infringers for the remaining claim supported by non-settling co-infringers.
- The third rule implements a subsidiary liability of the settling infringers when the non-settling co-infringers are not able to pay the damages that correspond to the remaining claim.

268. The § 2 of article 18 simply states that:

> *"When determining the contribution of each co-infringer, national courts shall take due account of any prior consensual settlement involving the relevant co-infringer."*

269. U.S. experience. Assuming that consensual settlements are an efficient alternative way to end disputes between competition law infringers and their victims, these propositions may be regarded as useful. They will probably persuade the infringers to compensate the victims in an out-of-court negotiation. The U.S. experience provides interesting data in this trendy way to solve antitrust litigation. (see *supra* § 17). But if settlements seem to be common in private antitrust litigation,[39] are they adapted to all kinds of disputes?

2. Are consensual settlements adapted to mass consumer litigation?

270. Principal-agent problems. A first reason to ask this question is the principal-agent problems. These well-known problems arise between the

[39] R. Whish, D. Bailey, *Competition Law*, 7th ed., Oxford University Press, 2012, pp. 315 to 316; C. Prieto, C. Si Bouazza, « Rapport spécial en droit de la concurrence », *in Réponse de Trans Europe Experts à la Consultation publique de la Commission européenne: « Renforcer la cohérence de l'approche européenne en matière de recours collectifs »*, 2011, p. 24 *sqq.*, at, p. 27; C. Piché, « Recours collectif québécois : état des lieux », *in Sur la voie de l'action de groupe, Gazette du Palais*, 16 may 2013, n° 136, p. 11 *sqq.*

lawyers and their plaintiffs when the lawyers, acting as representative parties, can monitor the proceedings at their sole interest.[40] The most famous example of this risk is given by the U.S. class action litigation. It is not unusual there that the lawyers manage to secure their gains and limit the time spent on a case by accepting an early settlement. This strategy grants them a high per hour remuneration in contingency fees. However, the represented party only get low-value "coupons" from the defendants for price reductions on future purchases. Therefore, the compensation is below what it would have been if the trial had resulted in a final judgment.[41] Sometimes it is seen as the result of the lawyers' strategy to take advantage of the length and the cost of civil proceedings to convince the plaintiffs to end quickly with judicial spiral.[42] As Mr Leslie noted, for this reason:

> *"the efficacy of class action litigation as a means of enforcing antitrust laws is becoming increasingly suspect, as some class counsel rush to secure settlements that ensure a significant payout for the attorneys but leave the class significantly undercompensated and allow antitrust violators to retain much of their ill-gotten gains. This undermines the deterrent effect of private lawsuits and, consequently, of antitrust laws more broadly."*[43]

271. Risks of undercompensation. This abuse in settlements proceedings to the detriment of the represented parties is one of the concerns that the Class Action Fairness Act 2005 aimed to solve. This trend can be explained by the asymmetry of information between professionals lawyers and profane plaintiffs.[44] It could be a first reason to question the efficiency of settlements for the victims, especially consumers: they do not receive full compensation.[45]

272. Risks of undercompensation may also arise in asymmetric relationships between SME's and major firms. Indeed, contractual practices that reveal abuses of dominance will have little chance of being corrected through settlements. It is common sense: if the dominated victims do not

---

40 K. C. Wildfang, S. P. Slaughter, *op. cit.*, pp. 231 and 232.

41 A. Renda (ed.), J. Peysner, A. J. Riley, B. J. Rodger, *op. cit.*, pp. 279 and 280.

42 K. Roach, M. J. Trebilcock, "Private Enforcement of Competition Laws", *Osgoode Hall L. J.*, 1996, vol. 34(3), p. 461 *sqq.*, at p. 505.

43 C. R. Leslie, "De Facto Detrebling: The Rush To Settlement In Antitrust Class Action Litigation", *Ariz. L. Rev.*, 2008, vol. 50, p. 1009 *sqq.*, at p. 1010.

44 B. Deffains, « L'analyse économique de la résolution des conflits juridiques », *Revue française d'économie*, 1997, p. 57 *sqq.*, at p. 90.

45 C. R. Leslie, *op. cit.*, pp. 1015 and 1016.

even dare to go to court, it is hard to imagine that they could be able to impose a settlement to their powerful partner.

273. The full compensation objective. Is it a problem? The question may seem provocative if one subscribes to the unshakable assumption that private actions aim to compensate the damage suffered by the victims. But if we reverse this assumption to see private actions mainly as a medium to enhance repression and deterrence against unlawful conducts, the complaint would lose its acuity. It would then be possible to see in the – sometimes excessive – remuneration perceived by the lawyers a compensation for the services rendered to the community as private enforcers.[46] It is all about priorities.

274. In the context of European law, it seems as though that the *ratio legis* of the White Paper, of the June 11th 2013 directive proposal and of the majority of Member States law of tort placed on their short list of priorities the full compensation of damage. The instrumental economic analysis that would deem indifferent the destination of the illegal profit disgorged by the defendants would break too abruptly the balance of European laws. Despite the current renewal of private litigation in Europe which tends to be an instrument of deterrence and not only a way to provide corrective justice, full compensation for the damage will probably remain a priority. For this reason the principal-agent problems should raise serious concerns for European lawyers if consensual settlements grow in a near future.

275. Specific issues in mass consumer litigation. But the doubts that the development of consensual settlements may raise go further. The crucial importance of a quick dispute resolution is obvious when the victims are businesses. But is it really essential for a consumer whose interests are represented in collective action – and that does not even need to make the trip to the court – to save a few months through a settlement that will bring him probably less than a judgment? I doubt it.

276. In addition, it is true that a business, like a SME, has all the reasons to maintain a cordial and constructive relationship with a powerful infringer that was once its partner. This can justify it does not carry out a costly trial.[47] But for the consumer, it is utterly indifferent to keep such a good relationship with a private firm.

46 T. L. Russell, *op. cit.*, p. 157 and the authors quoted.
47 B. J. Rodger, "Private Enforcement of Competition Law, The Hidden Story", *op. cit.*, p. 111.

277. It is often argued that settlements would reduce legal risk by granting the victims modest compensation while avoiding the uncertainty of a trial.[48] But once again, the argument is not fully operative for consumers. Of course, the proof of an anticompetitive conduct remains uncertain. But if the defendant is guilty, we can hope that our judicial system will be able to design efficient solutions to allow the victims to establish this conduct and seek for appropriate remedies. Settlements should not be a palliative to the weaknesses of E.U. private law.

278. Economic argument. Moreover, the economic arguments that support settlements as a way to mitigate uncertainty are difficult to transpose to the European litigation. Just remember that they were conceived by North-American authors on the observation of the U.S. judicial model: the adversarial trial with discovery. But this model differs significantly from the continental civil proceedings. The costs it generates are incommensurately higher compared to those of the judicial systems of the Member States. The latter remain below those of a defendant sued in a U.S. court would have to pay.

279. To the economic argument of reducing legal uncertainty, I would much prefer a "lawyer's answer" to the one of an economist: the gray areas are hardly conceivable, at least for the obviously illegal conducts. If the defendant is guilty, the settlement could be seen as unfair because the consumer will not get any significant advantages from it. If the defendant is not guilty, the settlement will also be unfair because the consumer will get a compensation he did not deserve.

280. The costs of the judicial review of settlements. Assuming that settlements may be extended to mass consumer litigation, a judicial supervision will remain necessary to avoid the excesses of the U.S. systems (see *supra* § 19). Such supervisions will inevitably increase the costs of litigation.[49] If there is very few reliable data in France, the Barry Rodger study demonstrated that of 43 settlements between businesses, 22 of them were made after the dispute had been brought in court (see *infra* table E). Let's say that the costs of these aborted trials is still lower than the one of trials where a final judgment is rendered, the benefits of settlements remains though modest if the parties seize the judge in 50% of the cases before ending their dispute by a settlement.

[48] L. T. Sorkin, *op. cit.*, p. 576.

[49] S. Guinchard, « L'accès au juge. Le point de vue du juriste », *in* D. Cohen (ed.), *Droit et économie du procès civil*, *op. cit.*, p. 25 *sqq.*, at p. 31.

Table 17 – Barry Rodger Study

Table 1: Number and period of settlements				Table 7: Proceedings raised prior to settlement		
Year	**Frequency**	**Per cent**	**Valid per cent**	**Prior proceedings**	**Frequency**	**Per cent**
2000	3	7.0	7.1			
2001	4	9.3	9.5	Yes	22	51.2
2002	7	16.3	16.7			
2003	6	14.0	14.3			
2004	8	18.6	19.0	No	21	48.8
2005	14	32.6	33.3			
Total	42	97.7	100.0			
Missing	1	2.3	-	Total	43	100.0
Total	43	100.0	-			

Table 9: Basis of settlement			Table 21: Uncertainty of litigation		
Basis of settlement	**Frequency**	**Per cent**	**Uncertainty**	**Frequency**	**Per cent**
Payment in lieu of damages	10	23.3			
Agreement as to future conduct	12	27.9	Yes	24	55.8
A combination of both	9	20.9	No	19	44.2
Withdrawal of claim without any of the above	5	11.6	Total	43	100.0
Other	7	16.3			
Total	43	100.0			

B. J., Rodger, "Private Enforcement of Competition Law, The Hidden Story: Competition Litigation Settlements in the United Kingdom, 2000-2005", *ECLR*, 2008, 29(2), p. 96 et s.

3. Are opt-out consensual settlements the future of alternative dispute resolution?

281. The Dutch *collectieve afwikkeling massaschade*. Perhaps the best solution will come from the Netherlands. Since its creation in 2005, the Dutch opt-out settlement model (the *collectieve afwikkeling massaschade*) draws attention.[50] Its statistics are impressive and it results in massive settlements:

- 35 million euros in the Des case,
- 1 billion euro in the Dexia case,
- 352.6 million US$ in the Royal Dutch Shell.[51]

282. As recalled by the LIDC,[52] with whom we can share the interest in this device, the settlement is made by a representative on behalf of all 'possible' victims, so identified or identifiable. Once approved by a judge, the settlement binds all the victims represented. They can then collect the compensation they deserve unless they express their will not to be bound by the settlement. In this case, they have a limited time to sue the defendant in an individual action or to seek individual settlement. This *collectieve afwikkeling massaschade* creates a sort of opt-out settlement under judicial supervision. The mechanism has already proven its efficiency in remarkable cases, reflecting the attractiveness of the Dutch law.

283. Inspired by this model, the British government has also proposed in January 2013 the creation of a similar device, under the supervision of the Competition Appeal Tribunal (CAT). The CAT will have first to "certify" this process. If it deems appropriate to the dispute, then it will supervise the terms of the settlement to ensure that it is:

> *"fair, just and reasonable'; in other words, [...] it give[s] satisfactory recompense to those who have suffered loss, taking into account both the degree of loss alleged and the likelihood of a collective actions claim succeeding."*[53]

284. Mixing opt-in and opt-out. Once again, the same observations as those expressed before for group actions (see *supra* §§ 6 to 9) may apply here: both opt-in and opt-out settlements could be useful depending on the type of litigation. The court in charge of certifying the settlement could choose the appropriate model of representation.

285. Extending this dual settlements model all across Europe could be an interesting solution to rebalance the relationship between professionals

---

50 A. Maton, V. Poopalasingam, M. Kuijper, T. Angerbauer, "The Effectiveness of National Fora in Europe for the Practice of Antitrust Litigation", *J. European Competition Law & Practice*, 2012, vol. 3(6), p. 586 *sqq*.

51 R. Gaudet, *op. cit.*, p. 114.

52 LIDC, *Comments on the Commission's White Paper*, 2008, p. 6, available at: http://ec.europa.eu/competition/antitrust/actionsdamages/white_paper_comments/lidc_en.pdf

53 Dept. for Business Innovation & Skills, *op. cit.*, point 6.23.

and consumers. In this respect, the court's supervision would be necessary at the very beginning of the dispute resolution process. It could also be needed at the end of this process when the parties have concluded an agreement.

Section (IV): Incentive devices: Private funding? Public funding? Both?

1. May group action systems work in E.U. Member States without punitive damages and contingency fees?

286. Contingency fees in the U. S. As Mr Foer summed up:

> *"The institution of contingent fees for plaintiff's attorney plays a special role in antitrust litigation. The plaintiff is often not in a position to pay substantial fees based on hourly rates [...] the attorney has to take the case based on a cost/benefit analysis. [...] Plaintiff's attorneys in the US function much like syndications of venture capitalists. Typically, they diversify their portfolio in the expectation that most cases they take will lose but that the winning cases will pay off in a big way."*[54]

287. The winning cases will pay off "in a bigger way" regarding the fact that the amount of contingency fees will be based on a percentage of the treble damages awarded. That is why Mr Foer concludes by stating that:

> *"If private enforcement is to be effective, both prospective plaintiffs and their attorneys need to have a way to finance litigation. The contingent fee based on treble the actual damages has been a successful mechanism in the US, as reflected in the fact that more than 90 percent of antitrust cases are private".*[55]

288. This assertion convinces that treble damages are essential for the balance of the U.S. private enforcement model.[56]

---

54 A. A. Foer, "The Ideal Model for Private Enforcement of Competition Law", *in* J. Basedow, J. P. Terhechte, L. Tichy (ed.), *Private Enforcement of Competition Law*, Nomos, 2011, p. 203 *sqq.*, at p. 215.

55 *Ibid.*, p. 216.

56 E. D. Cavanagh, *op. cit.*, p. 635: "*trebling makes it unlikely that antitrust violators will profit from their wrongdoing. Theoretically, trebling is not necessary to bring about disgorgement of ill-gotten gains because plaintiffs' actual damages would presumably correspond to defendants' actual illicit gains. However, the reality is that plaintiffs are unlikely to invest the time and money in prosecuting a lengthy, complicated, and expensive civil antitrust*

289. Moreover, contingency fees are also seen as a stimulating device for lawyers to properly defend their clients as regard to the amounts perceived by law firms (see *infra* table F). As noted:

> *"This type of arrangement creates an incentive for the attorney to obtain a favorable result at a lower cost to all clients. Under incentive-based fee arrangement, an attorney's fees are dependent upon the result – the more favorable the settlement or judgment, the more fees collected by the attorney. Thus, in this type of arrangement, an attorney is given an incentive to resolve the lawsuit for the lowest possible cost to the client."*[57]

290. So a basic question arises: may the European private enforcement work without these two U.S. rooted devices: treble damages and contingency fees?

Table 18 – Lande-Davis Study

Table 7A: Percentage of Recovery Awarded as Attorney's Fees for Recoveries Less than $100 Million	
Case ($ millions in the recovery)	*Attorney's Fee Percentage*
Airline Ticket Commission (86)	33.3
Augmentin (91)	21.6 (weighted average of direct (20%) and indirect (25%))
NCAA (74)	26.8
Remeron (75)	33.3
Platinol (50)	33.3
Remeron (75)	33.3
Taxol (66)	30
Drill Bits (53)	30.8
Polypropylene Carpet (50)	33.3
Sorbates (96)	22-33
Terazosin (74)	33.3
Microcrystalline Cellulose (50)	33.3

claim if their recovery is limited to actual damages. Without trebling, therefore, antitrust violators may not be sued and may be more likely to reap the benefits of their illegal conduct. Trebling, on the other hand, assures that antitrust violators will be denied the fruits of their misconduct, even if all the victims of their wrongdoing do not come forward to claim their rightful share of damages".

57 K. C. Wildfang, S. P. Slaughter, *op. cit.*, p. 229 quoting S. W. Jones, M. Beard Glover, "The Attack on Traditional Billing Practices", 1998, vol. 20, *U. Ark. Little Rock L. J.*, p. 293 *sqq.*

Specialty Steel (50)	30
Lysine (65)	7
Commercial Explosives (77)	30
Graphite Electrodes (47)	15

Table 7B: Percentage of Recovery Awarded as Attorney's Fees for Recoveries Between $100 Million and $500 Million	
Case (S millions in the recovery)	*Attorney's Fee Percentage*
Automative Refinishing Paint (106)	32-33.3
Buspirone (220)	33.3
Cardizem (110)	30
DRAM (326)	25
Flat Glass (122)	32
Linerboard (202)	30
Oil Lease (193)	25
Paxil (165)	20 & 30
Relafen (250)	33

Table 7C: Percentage of Recovery Awarded as Attorney's Fees for Recoveries Exceeding $500 Million	
Case {$ millions in the recovery)	*Attorney's Fee Percentage*
Visa/MasterCard (3,383)	6.5
Auction Houses (552)	5.2 (plaintiffs' attorneys got 20% of their fee in coupons—the same percentage that class members got of their recovery in coupons)
El Paso (1,427)	6
Fructose (531)	25
NASDAQ (1,027)	13

R. H. Lande, J. P. Davis, "Benefits From Private Antitrust Enforcement: An Analysis of Forty Cases", *USF L. Rev.*, 2008, vol. 42, p. 882 *sq.*

291. Concerns. The lack of effective funding in the EU is often denounced as one of the most serious pitfalls of the European private enforcement. Many studies in the matter addressed this question.[58] But how the costs

58 See e. g. H. Andersson, E. Legnerfält, "Effective private enforcement: The Swedish experience, a lesson for the EU?", *Concurrences*, n° 3-2009, p. 156 *sqq.*, at p. 161; J. Peysner, "Costs and Financing in Private Third Party Competition Damages Actions", *Comp. L. Rev.*, 2006, vol. 3,

will be covered if EU Member States forbid lawyers to "kickstart" litigation by funding the actions?[59] The concern appears for follow-on actions but above all for stand-alone actions. As stated:

> *"If no mechanism is established, regardless of what it looks like, litigation in antitrust law would perhaps be reduced to follow-on actions".*[60]

292. We have seen before that the outcome of stand-alone actions to the efficiency of private enforcement should not be denied (see *supra* § 12). Thus, E.U. litigation needs devices to fund the victims actions that otherwise will not be brought to court.

293. European business models. Despite their major support to the efficiency of private enforcement in the U.S., contingency fees are unlikely to be adopted all across Europe.[61] Nonetheless, some business models similar to the contingency fees system already exist in Europe. For instance, private insurers could replace "lawyers-entrepreneurs" in the process. They could accept the risk generated by the legal uncertainty of private enforcement and then being remunerated by an amount of the award settled or granted by the court. This option still remains theoretical and Mr Peysner expressed a dubious appreciation of this private way to fund litigation:

> *"Competition claims like all commercial litigation are one-off cases so litigation insurers are likely to be more risk averse and at best conservative on setting premium levels which may make them uneconomic."*[62]

294. Therefore, the solution is more likely to come from private "litigation entrepreneurs". Some company already attempted to build a business model that allows them to fund private enforcement while earning money.

---

p. 97 *sqq.*; K. Roach, M. J. Trebilock, *op. cit.*, p. 504; L. Rozon, *op. cit.*, p. 58; T. L. Russell, *op. cit.*, p. 178; D. Wilsher, "The Public Aspects of Private Enforcement in EC law: Some Constitutional and Administrative Challenges of a Damages Culture", *Comp. L. Rev.*, 2006, vol. 3, p. 27 *sqq.*, at pp. 36 and 37; A. Renda (dir.), J. Peysner, A. J. Riley, B. J. Rodger *et al.*, *op. cit.*, p. 178.

59 E. D. Cavanagh, *op. cit.*, p. 648: *"Without some adjustment in current litigation practices of European courts to permit access to attorneys by private antitrust plaintiffs, the private right of action may never get off the ground."*

60 H.-W. Micklitz, *op. cit.*, p. 117.

61 G. Berrisch, E. Jordan, R. S. Roldan, "E.U. Competition And Private Actions For Damages", *Northwestern J. Int. Law and Business*, 2004, p. 585 *sqq.*, at p. 598.

62 J. Peysner, *op. cit.*, p. 99.

295. The Cartel Damages Claims (CDC) company is probably the most famous. Presenting itself as the *"frontrunner of private antitrust enforcement in Europe"*,[63] its model aims to outsource the claims enforcement. As the CDC highlights on its website,[64] four main qualities can be attached to this model:

- The claim is handled by experts, so the chances of success may be higher.
- The bundling of claims allows cooperation with different victims and the wider collection of data. This can help to build accurate counterfactual analyses to prove the exact amount of damages suffered by the victims. The bundling also put pressure on the defendants and could convince him to settle.
- The outsourcing of claims enforcement reduces the strain on commercial relationships with the cartelists.
- This is a new business opportunity that may attract investment.

296. This private funding could be a helpful option to replace in Europe the U.S. contingency fees system.

2. Is public funding a sustainable alternative to private funding?

297. Mixing private and public funding. It is possible that private agents will be reluctant to carry on the riskiest actions alone. The funding of such actions through private devices – such as private litigation funders – could be insufficient. That is the reason why it could be necessary to share the financial risks of uncertain litigation with public funders. Such a risk repartition could favor the triggering of actions less likely to succeed.

298. Quebec's experience. The proposal to rely on public funding in order to encourage private enforcement is not new. It has been proposed by authors inspired by the Quebec's *Fonds d'aide aux recours collectifs* whose success seems engaging.[65] Creating such a public fund was also suggested by the French proposal of *loi Chatel*, which was not adopted. Its

---

[63] http://www.carteldamageclaims.com/

[64] http://www.carteldamageclaims.com/Creating%20Incentives.shtml

[65] Such public funds also exist in Hong-Kong, Australia or Ontario in Canada: A. Renda (ed.), J. Peysner, A. J. Riley, B. J. Rodger *et al.*, *op. cit.*, p. 621 to 623; and in Brazil: A. Gidi, "Class Actions in Brazil – A Model for Civil Law Countries", *Am. J. Comparative Law*, vol. 51, 2003, p. 307 *sqq.*, at pp. 339 et 340.

range, however, was limited to violations of consumer law. But the idea was good and should be extended to competition litigation. The Quebec law provides then a complete model that proved not only its efficiency, but also its assimilation by a judicial tradition whose roots lay both in the Civil and in the Common law traditions. This is not a small advantage in the context of a possible implementation at the European level.[66] How could these public fund work?

299. Applicants' eligibility. The first question to be resolved is the applicants' eligibility for funding. Some basic criteria should be sufficient to lay the foundations for a sustainable and equitable system. Following the Quebec-style system, applicants could obtain funding if they meet two conditions:

- they are able to demonstrate the need for public funding,
- their action is not frivolous and may succeed.

300. The first criterion is to be assessed in the light of the financial standing of the applicant, the specifics characters of the case and the likely costs this case requires. The second criterion could be implemented by a test measuring the reasonable chances of success that could determine whether or not the case should be funded. This test could be flexible in order to coincide with the public fund's endowment. If the fund has sufficient resources to afford fails, then the "reasonable" criterion will be appreciated smoothly and vice versa in times of restraint.

301. In case of refusal to grant funding, some judicial remedies should be opened to the applicant. Once the amount is provided, the fund may then pay lawyers' fees, expert fees, costs, expenses incurred by the amicus curiae's consultation, notification to members of the group etc.[67]

302. Financing the fund. The second question for which we must try to provide some short answers is that of financing the fund. Once again, the Quebec-style system is helpful. It advocates the possibility to subrogate the fund in the applicant's rights by allowing it to recover its expenses to the defendant.

---

66 A. Renda (ed.), J. Peysner, A. J. Riley, B. J. Rodger *et al.*, *op. cit.*, p. 625. "*From a European perspective the Quebec solution appears at first sight more appropriate, with a possible extension of the scope of the mechanism to include all antitrust civil actions and not just class actions.*"

67 *Id.* "*The Fonds pays the assisted person or persons attorney fees and expert's fees and other incidental expenses; offering vital cash flow as the case proceeds and replacing the firm's bank or the partners' capital in a US plaintiff litigation firm.*"

303. In addition, external funding may complete this first way to finance the fund. At the end of the collective litigation and after a delay to be defined, the damages unclaimed by the victims may be awarded to the fund. It may also be necessary to take a set percentage of the total amounts recovered by the victims.

304. Article 42 of the Quebec law on collective redress could be a good model to inspire European legislation:

> *"42. In the case of a collective recovery of the claims, the Fonds shall withhold a percentage fixed by regulation of the Government on the balance established under article 1033 or 1034 of the Code of Civil Procedure; in other cases, the Fonds shall withhold a percentage fixed by regulation of the Government on every liquidated claim."*[68]

305. It would also be possible to allocate to the fund a portion of the criminal and civil penalties imposed in cases of consumer or competition litigation or even use the *cy-près* doctrine.

306. The British OFT expressed its interest for the *cy-près* doctrine in a 2007 report:

> *"If the proceeds are not completely distributed to individual consumers, this raises the question of how to dispose of the remaining funds. One option would be to allow the court to direct how the fund should be used for the benefit of consumers falling within the category (or, failing that, consumers more generally). This is generally known as cy pres. The fund could, for instance, be used for consumer education or research or to finance other representative actions. Public bodies may be able to make suggestions to the court as to how those cy pres powers should be used. The extent of courts' involvement in management (bearing in mind effective use of resource) and the costs of managing such funds would need to be considered carefully."*[69]

307. If needed, nothing should prevent the fund administrators from applying for a bank loan or seeking public funding from Member State governments or the European institutions.

---

68 *Loi sur les recours collectifs*, available in English at: http://canlii.org/en/qc/laws/stat/rsq-c-r-2.1/latest/rsq-c-r-2.1.html

69 OFT, *Private actions in competition law: effective redress for consumers and business*, 2007, pt 4.37, available at: http://www.oft.gov.uk/shared_oft/reports/comp_policy/oft916.pdf

308. Thus, this set of proposals mixing private and public funding are inspired by successful experiences. They should contribute to the effectiveness of private enforcement. Now the ball is in the E.U. legislators' court…

309. Concluding remarks. To each question addressed in this research paper, a cautious response has been made. Rather than making unbending choices and dismiss devices inspired by the U.S. experience, it seems preferable to retain a plurality of options. It is especially obvious for the question of collective redress: no option should be ruled out peremptorily on behalf of a supposed "European legal culture". In this matter, the observation of EU Member States laws reveal the absence of a sole European pattern or a common core of rules.[70]

310. Mr Foer and Mr Cuneo concluded a remarkable book on the topic by noting that there was no ideal model of private enforcement.[71] This is precisely for this reason that only a wide-ranging set of legal devices can be helpful to cope with the variety of private litigation. Definitely, to head towards an unreachable ideal model, plurality is the only key.

---

70 J. G. Delatre, *op. cit.*, p. 38: "*The reality is that, although some similarities exist, a close examination of the collective redress mechanisms available in Europe shows a complete lack of discernable pattern on which to base a proposal. There is a lack of homogeneity in procedural law and the widest range of mechanisms available to European consumers. Those mechanisms range from the far reaching Portuguese popular action, the closest equivalent in Europe to the US class action, to mechanisms with a strictly limited scope, whether procedurally or substantively, such as the Dutch and German procedure.*" (p. 37).

71 A. A. Foer, J. W. Cuneo, "Toward an effective system of private enforcement", *in* A. A. Foer, J. W. Cuneo (ed.), *The International Handbook on Private Enforcement of Competition Law*, Edward Elgar, 2010, p. 590 *sqq.*, at pp. 592 and 593.

PART II: COLLECTIVE REDRESS: THE GROUP AND THE JUDICIAL SUPERVISION OF THE SETTLEMENT

VINCENT SMITH*

311. This short commentary seeks to develop the points made at the GCLC conference in November 2013 in Brussels in the above session. It addresses two issues which appear to have been overlooked in the European Commission's reform package – specifically in the Commission recommendation on collective redress.[1]

312. The first issue is how and when to determine – regardless of whether the claim is of the recommended 'opt-in' variety, or the 'exceptional' opt-out variety – who is in the group which the representative body represents. Should a representative body only be entitled to act on behalf of its members, or should the represented group be wider?

313. The second issue is judicial supervision not only of the contractual terms of any settlement (the issues here are highlighted in Dr Amaro's paper in this collection),[2] but also of the method and practice of distribution of the settlement payment.

314. There appear to be three issues in the practice of settlement distribution which any system of collective redress will need to address:

1. making sure that adequate notice is given to the group;
2. ensuring that any person claiming compensation falls within the definition of the group for whose benefit the settlement has been

---

* V. SMITH, Partner, Sheppard & Co, London.

1 COMMISSION RECOMMENDATION of 11 June 2013 on common principles for injunctive and compensatory collective redress mechanisms in the Member States concerning violations of rights granted under Union Law (2013/396/EU), OJ L201/60, 26.7.2013 ("Recommendation")

2 Research Paper: Collective redress, consensual settlements and other incentive devices – plurality is the key – Dr Rafael Amaro, January 2014

made (which is closely linked to the first issue raised above – defining the 'class');

3. dealing with the residue of the fund (if any) after the period for distribution has closed and the expenses of the litigation have been paid.

Section (I): Who is represented?

315. The Commission Recommendation envisages a system of collective redress based on the bringing of action by non-profit representative bodies. The question arises as to whom those bodies represent. The most basic solution would be to limit participation in a collective action to those persons who are members of the body in question. This would have the benefit of certainty for both the body, the defendant and the supervising court, as eligibility could easily be checked by reference to the body's membership list.

316. However, this is not the solution which the Recommendation appears to adopt. Although not expressly excluded by the wording of the Recommendation, a membership requirement appears inconsistent with the requirement that, in cross-border cases, courts recognise the standing of representative bodies established in other Member States.[3] Almost all of the bodies which the Recommendation envisages might bring a collective action are national in scope and their members will normally be residents of a single Member State. There would therefore be little purpose in the Recommendation making specific provision for cross-border situations if collective actions were limited to existing members of representative bodies.

317. There is also a practical objection. Most bodies which are not-for-profit nevertheless have a subscription requirement for membership. Requiring victims of mass harm caused by breaches of directly applicable EU law to subscribe to membership of a collective body before they can claim compensation (especially if the membership dues exceed the likely amount of compensation) appears – at best – counter-intuitive and likely to impede access to justice.

[3] Recommendation, paras. 17 and 18.

318. On the basis that the representative body must be able to represent victims other than its members, how wide does the Recommendation envisage that Member States should allow the net to be cast? It is suggested that the Recommendation might fail in its basic aim of setting a common framework for collective redress in the EU if it leaves too much discretion to the Member States. However, the Recommendation is in this regard imprecise: it defines a 'representative action;[4]

(d) "representative action" means an action which is brought by a representative entity, [...] on behalf and in the name of two or more natural or legal persons who claim to be exposed to the risk of suffering harm or to have been harmed in a mass harm situation [...];

and provides that those person may be represented by a body where:[5]

(b) there [is] a direct relationship between the main objectives of the entity and the rights granted under Union law that are claimed to have been violated in respect of which the action is brought;

319. So the only limitations recommended by the Commission are that the persons represented should (or should be at risk of) suffering harm from the same event, that that event constitutes a violation of directly effective EU law and that the body representing them should have objects which relate directly to the EU law provision alleged to have been infringed.

320. There is therefore no requirement that the represented persons should have suffered the same type of harm (so both physical and moral loss, as well as more general pecuniary loss could be claimed), nor that they be seeking the same legal remedy (so a single collective action could claim both damages and an injunction on behalf of sub-groups of claimants), nor even that the action be brought in a single court (although the EU law on civil jurisdiction and enforcement[6] may in practice prevent multiple 'mirror' claims by the same group).

321. And the requirement that the objects of the representative body be 'directly' related to the EU law alleged to have been breached can also be expected to give rise to difficulty. Often the objects of not-for-profits may be very widely cast or vaguely interpreted. More importantly, the same event causing mass harm may infringe several directly effective EU law rights, some of which may be within the objects of one association or body and some of which may not. Does the Commission recommend that the

4 Recommendation para. 3(d)
5 Recommendation para. 4(b)
6 Regulation EC 44/2001of 22 December 2000, OJ L12/1 16.1.2001

losses due to harm caused by an action which breaches 'out-of scope' EU law should remain uncompensated while breaches of 'within scope' laws arising from the same event of mass harm will receive a remedy?

322. Clearly the recommendation leaves substantial latitude to Member States as to how (or indeed, given this document's current status, whether) to introduce collective redress mechanisms into their national civil procedure rules. However, given this wide latitude in defining who may participate in a collective action, it appears quite probable that the Recommendation may fail in its aim of setting a coherent framework for collective redress in the EU.

Section (II): Supervising the method of settlement distribution

323. The result of giving a large discretion to member States is a likely wide latitude to be allowed to settling parties (defendants and representative bodies) in the EU in defining the scope of the group to whom any settlement applies. Judicial supervision of collective redress settlements therefore appears entirely indispensable. Of course, given that the Recommendation prefers an 'opt-in' model, the ultimate test of the acceptability of a settlement will normally be whether large numbers within the intended target group in fact freely choose to opt in by making a claim against the settlement fund. But it is suggested that this is not a complete answer to the issues raised here: not least as 'opt-out' mechanisms continue to be permitted and many exist within the EU.

1. Notice to the represented group

324. The Recommendation expressly addresses Member State rules on publicity for these kinds of claims.[7] Rules which prevent (such as the French legislation preventing solicitation for litigation) or hinder advertising to claimants will need to be amended. However, given the wideness of the discretion allowed to the settling parties as to the scope of the settlement, the description of the settlement and, crucially here, who is allowed to claim under it, will need close judicial scrutiny.

7 Recommendation paras. 10-12

325. Lack of or even imprecision in describing the eligibility criteria to apply for payment under the settlement may lead to victims losing out on compensation. Even in an opt-in system, a delay in deciding whether a particular claimant is entitled could lead to loss if a relevant limitation period expired in the meantime. And for opt-out systems, where all claims within the scope of the class will become barred at the conclusion of the collective redress action, precision in defining those claims which are within the action is self-evidently essential.

326. Inevitably, this will mean that civil courts in the EU will need to engage directly with and approve the drafting of the relevant notices – the public interest principles at stake here are too important to be left to the discretion of the settling parties, it is suggested. In practice the scope of the action will not be described finally in the claims made at the commencement of the claim, but will be set by the terms of the notice of settlement (or the terms of the redress action judgment if there is no settlement): in particular it is this notice which will in practice at least define the *res judicata* effect of the collective redress action.

2. Ensuring that claimants fall within the class

327. Even where the notice gives a firm definition of who is (and is not) entitled to claim against the settlement or compensation fund, the administration of payments to eligible victims is of substantial legal as well as practical importance.

328. The distribution of the fund is unlikely to be carried out directly by the supervising court except in cases where there are very few members in an opt-in group claim. Rather, where there are a large number of entitled claimants, the distribution of the fund is very likely to be outsourced. A possibility would be to entrust the task of distributing the settlement proceeds to the representative body having brought the claim: this assumes that it has the resources and expertise to carry out this task which in many cases will not be the case. In other cases a third party 'trustee' will need to be appointed to distribute the compensation.

329. In either case, the supervising court will need to be vigilant both at the time that the distribution 'trustee' is selected and also ongoing, that the distribution process is being carried out correctly. In particular the evidential burden on claimants to show that they fit within the description set out in the notice should not be set either too high (which would discourage meritorious applicants) nor too low (which would encourage frivolous ones). It should always be open to the supervising court to give directions to the trustee or to replace him.

330. The dangers of thin court supervision of the distribution process for both defendants and victims are starkly shown by two recent examples. In the *Deepwater Horizon* disaster settlement, the defendant, BP had to seek a review of the actions of the US court appointed settlement trustee after he allegedly set the evidential requirements for claimants applying against the settlement fund too low,[8] making payments where there was no loss and increasing substantially the cost of the settlement to BP. And in the *Trafiguera* case, the award of the English court, paid to compensate victims of an environmental pollution catastrophe in Cote d'Ivoire, was allegedly diverted by the distribution trustee, leaving the victims substantially out of pocket.[9]

3. Unclaimed settlement proceeds

331. Given the Recommendation's position that the 'opt-in' model of collective redress should be the EU norm, the issue of unclaimed settlement ought not to be significant: to the extent that there are not claims, the settling defendant will not make payment. However, at least where the take-up of the settlement is lower than expected by the settling parties – and arguably in all cases – the full costs of representation of the claimant group and of distributing the settlement should be borne by the settling defendant to ensure that the claimants receive full compensation as required by EU law.[10]

332. Where opt-out collective redress is permitted, the question of how to deal with the unclaimed part of any compensation fund at the end of the process has been much debated.[11] We would simply note here the solution proposed by the UK government in the Bill[12] currently (January 2014) before Parliament to introduce opt-out collective actions for competition claims. It provides that, in the event that there are unclaimed funds after the period for distributing the compensation has expired, the Competition

8 http://www.ft.com/cms/s/0/16525a28-7ab0-11e3-80ff-00144feabdc0.html#axzz2rhoBbFep

9 http://www.amnesty.org/en/news-and-updates/côte-d'ivoire-missing-millions-must-reach-trafigura-toxic-waste-victims-2011-08

10 See for example, Recommendation para. 30, for a reiteration of the principle.

11 See for one example, Amaro, *op.cit.*, pp. 22-24.

12 Consumer Rights Bill 24 January 2014, see schedule 8 para 6., at http://www.publications.parliament.uk/pa/bills/cbill/2013-2014/0161/14161.pdf

Appeal Tribunal *must* make those funds over to the government-run *pro bono* scheme for litigation funding for parties otherwise unable to afford access to justice – there is no discretion. The Bill does not set down the same requirement for unclaimed funds after a settlement – the parties can, presumably agree what they wish in this regard (including reversion to the defendant) – which could create some incentive for the defendant to reach a settlement agreement before trial.

Conclusion

333. By allowing Member States and, by extension, settling parties great latitude in setting the scope of a collective action and on how (as well as to whom) awards of compensation may be distributed, the Recommendation runs a significant risk of failing in its aim of setting out a common framework for collective redress in the EU and of ensuring that victims of mass harm resulting from EU law breaches are fully compensated.

334. It is to be hoped that, in the light of experience in the application of the principles in the Recommendation, the Commission will feel able to complement its current provisions with more detail on the all-important "back-end" of the process for EU collective redress, to ensure that it works properly and to the full benefit of European citizens throughout the Union.

III

DETERMINING LIABILITY

PART I: QUANTIFICATION ISSUES: ESTIMATING AND CALCULATING HARM, PRESUMPTION OF HARM IN CARTEL CASES

■

Pascale Déchamps*, **

Section (I): The new draft Directive[1] from the European Commission and general approach to estimating damages

1. Estimating damages within the context of European law

335. The EU law compensatory principles are now well established in case law.[2] In this context, the Commission has drafted a new Directive aimed at formalising these principles and empowered the national courts with the means to enforce them in an effective way. In the context of the June 2013 draft Directive (hereafter, the 'draft Directive'), Article 16 deals with quantification of harm in two paragraphs:

> *1. Member States shall ensure that, in the case of a cartel infringement, it shall be presumed that the infringement caused harm. The infringing undertaking shall have the right to rebut this presumption.*

---

* This paper largely builds on three Oxera documents: a study for the European Commission on damages quantification (*Quantifying antitrust damages, towards non-binding guidance for courts*, Oxera *et al.*, Report for the European Commission, December 2009), an Oxera Agenda article of September 2012 (*What's driving damages? The* 2 Travel v Cardiff Bus *competition law ruling*) and an Oxera agenda article of July 2013 (*The EU draft Damages Actions Directive: another rebuttable presumption to rebut?*). However, the views expressed here are those of the author only.

** P. Dechamps, Senior Adviser at Oxera.

1 Proposal for a Directive of the European parliament and of the council on certain rules governing for damages under national law for infringements of the competition law provisions of the Member States and of the European Union, 2013/0185 (COD), 11 June 2013, thereafter the 'draft Directive'.

2 See, for example, joined cases C-295/04 to C-298/04, Judgment of the Court of Justice of 13 July 2006, known as the 'Manfredi judgment'.

> *2. Member States shall ensure that the burden and the level of proof and of fact-pleading required for the quantification of harm does not render the exercise of the injured party's right to damages practically impossible or excessively difficult. Member States shall provide that the court be granted the power to estimate the amount of harm.*

336. The Directive specifies explicitly that victims are entitled to full compensation (for example, at Article 2) and that the courts should have the power to estimate damages (Article 16).

337. Published alongside the Directive was a Communication from the Commission on quantifying damages,[3] to be read in conjunction with a practical guide to quantifying harm in actions for damages (hereafter, the 'Practical guide').[4] This Practical guide is based extensively on the Oxera et al. report prepared for the Commission in 2009 (hereafter the 'Oxera et al. study').[5]

338. Yet, national systems and rules still apply: the Commission's 'suggestions' do not supersede national rules, unless these rules do not allow for full compensation of harm.

2. General approach to estimating damages

339. The general approach to estimating damages, which goes beyond estimating damages in the context of infringements of antitrust law, always relies on answering a seemingly simple question: what would have happened had the conduct not taken place?

340. This hypothetical situation, in which the practice has not taken place, is called a 'benchmark' or a 'counterfactual' or 'but-for' situation. It cannot be directly observed or measured, yet needs to be precisely defined in order to estimate actual harm. Once the benchmark has been agreed on, harm is estimated in the following way: first, the difference between actual profits and the benchmark level of profits is calculated on a per-unit

---

3 Communication from the Commission on quantifying harm in actions for damages based on breaches of Article 101 or 102 of the Treaty on the Functioning of the European Union, 13 June 2013.

4 Commission staff working document, Practical guide, Quantifying harm in actions for damages based on breaches of Article 101 or 102 of the Treaty on the Functioning of the European Union, 6 June 2013.

5 *Quantifying antitrust damages, towards non-binding guidance for courts*, Oxera *et al.*, Report for the European Commission, December 2009.

basis; then this unit 'overcharge' or 'lost profit' is multiplied by quantities to obtain a monetary amount; and finally, interest is applied.

341. How the benchmark should be constructed is frequently crucial to any damages case, since it directly determines how large damage claims can be.

3. Estimating harm from cartels and exclusionary conducts

342. Generally speaking, victims of anti-competitive behaviour are entitled to compensation for:[6]

- actual loss suffered (*damnum emergens*)—for example, higher advertising costs incurred as a way to compensate for an exclusionary conduct;
- loss of profits (*lucrum cessans*)—i.e. the additional profits that would have been made absent the behaviour (for example, higher profit margins absent the exclusionary conduct);
- interest (see section (IV) below).

343. The first two categories are typically lumped together under the term 'loss of profits' (see, for example, paragraph 183 of the Practical guide).

344. In cartel cases, irrespective of the way the cartel operated (i.e. irrespective of whether the cartel involved price-fixing, market sharing, lower investment, etc.), damages may result from:

- a price overcharge: absent the cartel, the price charged in the market would have been lower—customers therefore paid too much for the goods and suffered harm;
- possibly fewer volumes traded:[7] because of the high price, customers ended up buying lower volumes, or perhaps not buying at all. In the case of customers buying the goods as inputs to their own production or distribution process, these additional foregone quantities would potentially have resulted in higher profits for the customers downstream.

345. Figure 5 illustrates these two effects. Absent the cartel, the customer would have bought quantities Q_1 at a price of P_1. As a result of a price rise

6 Draft Directive, Article 2, para. 2.

7 This effect is generally considered as an effect of secondary order relative to the price effect and can be particularly difficult to estimate.

imposed by the cartel, the customer ends up buying quantity Q_2 at a price of P_2. $P_2 - P_1$ is the so-called 'overcharge'. Area A is the difference between the price imposed by the cartel (P_2) and the price that should have prevailed (P_1) over the quantities bought under the cartel price (Q_2) – this is the overcharge over all quantities actually purchased. Area B represents the 'volume effect': absent the cartel, the customer would have bought $Q_1 - Q_2$ additional quantities because prices would have been more attractive. These additional quantities may have led to higher profits made by the customer, for example, if the customer is a distributor of the goods.

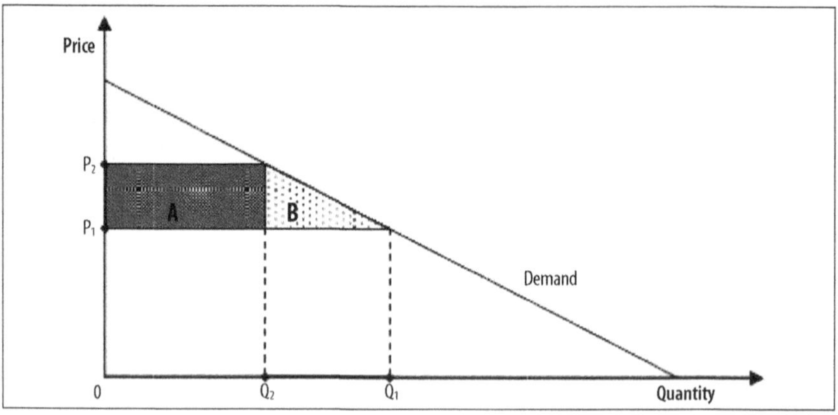

Figure 5: Effect of cartels price overcharge and volume effect

Source: 'Practical guide', paragraph 128.

346. In cases of exclusionary conduct, damages may result from the following.

- Actual lost profits: these are the difference between foregone revenues as a result of the practice and the variation in costs. For example, if a company was excluded from a market and would have made revenues of €10 absent the practice, the foregone revenue is €10 but the amount of damage is not €10. The damage is the lost profit, which takes into account costs of production that would have been incurred had these quantities actually been produced. In our example, if the costs incurred to reach revenues of €10 are €3, the actual lost profit is €7. If the victim incurred higher costs as a result of the practice (for example, higher advertising costs), they should be added to the amount of lost profits.
- Future losses? These may occur when companies cannot re-enter a market, or when the practice has had a lasting effect (for example, a reputational effect). In such circumstances, even after the practice has stopped, ongoing harm may be imposed on the victim. The ability to

claim damages for future losses is typically determined by national law, which also specifies how far in the future a victim can claim damages for. As a matter of economics, future losses need to be discounted, to take into account the loss in the value of money over time.

347. The remainder of this paper is structured as follows. Section II discusses the question of how to construct the benchmark situation when estimating damages. Section III discusses more specifically the presumption of harm in cartel cases as proposed in the draft Directive. Section IV explains in more detail how to go from the benchmark to calculating damage, with an emphasis on the ways to apply interest.

This paper does not discuss issues around passing-on of overcharges to downstream customers (and volume effects), estimating value of commerce or causation.

Section (II): How to construct the benchmark

348. Several methods, requiring different types of data, can be used to construct the benchmark. This section first presents the framework of analysis to which specific methodologies belong. It then describes more precisely a number of techniques that are commonly used: cross-sectional comparisons, before-during-after comparisons, difference-in-differences comparisons, financial-analysis-based techniques, and market structure-based analyses.

1. Classification of methods and models

349. Figure 6 presents a matrix, which forms the framework of analysis for determining the right counterfactual. The top panel of the matrix lists the different approaches that can be used, with the middle panel specifying, for each of these approaches, on which parameters the benchmark is constructed. Finally, the bottom panel of the matrix indicates the economic or econometric techniques that are used to compute the benchmark, using the elements listed in the middle panel, from the most simple to the most complex. Techniques can be more or less data-intensive.

350. Although this matrix may appear complex at first, the key message to be drawn from it is the fact that there is a wide range of methodologies available to compute a benchmark. In particular, when the amount or type of data available to each of the parties in a case is not the same (for example, due to limited document disclosure), parties may apply different yet equally appropriate techniques to estimate the right benchmark. Nevertheless, in practice, one or two methods will turn out to be the 'natural' methodologies for a specific context, depending on the type of infringement and the type of data available to undertake the analysis.

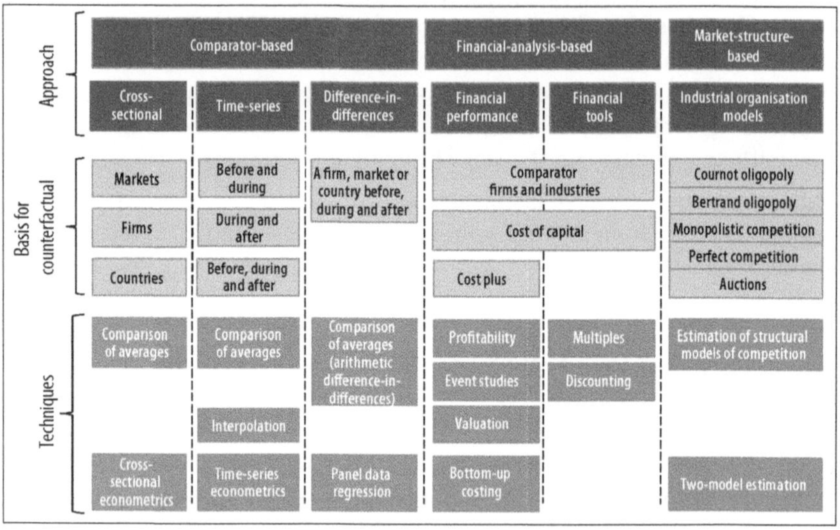

Figure 6: Framework of analysis for determining the right counterfactual

Source: Oxera.

2. Cross-sectional analysis

351. A so-called 'cross-sectional' analysis consists of comparing outcomes in the market affected by the infringement with outcomes in a market that has not been affected by the infringement. The idea is that a cartel, for example, would lead to higher prices in the market where it operates compared with what can be observed in a competitive market. In order to be relevant, the benchmark market used as a comparator needs to have characteristics that are similar to those of the affected market, but for the collusive behaviour. Benchmarks often used include neighbouring countries (or similar local markets), similar product markets or similar firms.

352. When running an international comparison, for example, a cross-sectional analysis involves comparing the price charged in a country where the infringement took place (for example, France) with prices charged in other countries (for example, Germany or the UK) at the same moment. If the price charged in France is higher than the price charged in Germany and the UK, the difference in price may be considered as the result of the collusive behaviour.

353. If this approach (comparison of averages) can provide a sense for the direction in which a damage estimation would go, care needs to be taken regarding whether the benchmark and affected markets are sufficiently similar that all of the price difference can be considered to result from the collusive behaviour. It may be the case, for example, that price differences result from exchange-rate issues (for example, when comparing France with the UK), or that different countries incur slightly different costs. If possible, it is therefore advisable to undertake some cross-sectional econometric analysis, which allows comparison of markets while controlling for legitimate differences in price expectations. In other words, econometric techniques make it possible to distinguish between price differences between markets that are the result of genuine market differences (independent from any collusive behaviour) and price differences that result from collusive behaviour.

3. Before-during-after analysis

354. The so-called 'before-after' (or 'before-during-after') comparison of prices has become relatively common, particularly in cartel cases. It belongs to the 'comparator-based' 'time-series' category of Figure 6.

355. The idea is to compare prices during the infringement period with prices that prevailed during a period that can be considered competitive. If prices during the infringement period are higher than prices during the benchmark period, the overcharge is computed as the difference between the two sets of prices.

356. The competitive period, which then becomes the benchmark, can take place before or after the infringement period, at least theoretically. For example, the period following dawn raids on companies has been considered as a relevant competitive benchmark in many cases. Periods before an infringement can constitute a more contestable benchmark, since it is possible that the cartel was already taking place before the official start of the infringement period (even though the companies, officially, have not been found guilty of an infringement during this earlier period).

357. On the basis of cartel member price variations over time, it is possible to compare prices during the infringement period with prices, say, after the infringement. This comparison can be very simple, such as a comparison of average prices charged during these two periods. In the case of data available before and after the infringement, a possibility is to interpolate prices—i.e. consider that prices during the infringement period should have followed the trend exhibited by prices before and after the infringement.

358. Figure 7 below provides an illustration of this technique: the figure shows the price charged by a cartelist over time (based on a real case), represented by the thick black line. This price increases steadily when the cartel is created, remains at a high level (with some variation) until the firm is dawn-raided, and then gradually decreases. A counterfactual based on interpolation consists of simply drawing a (dotted) line between actual prices during the 'before' period on the left and the 'after' period on the right, ignoring actual price variations during the cartel period.

359. In this example, and it is often the case, the actual price observed immediately after the dawn raids cannot be used as part of the benchmark, since prices tend to be affected by cartel behaviour some time after an infringement has ended. If prices remain high for a time after the dawn raids, prices in the benchmark period will be higher than the true but-for price, leading to underestimation of the overcharge. On the contrary, if prices after the dawn raids collapse due to price wars and go below long-term competitive prices, prices in the benchmark period may be lower than the true but-for price, leading to overestimation of the overcharge. Therefore, the benchmark needs to be based on prices observed some time after the cartel collapses.

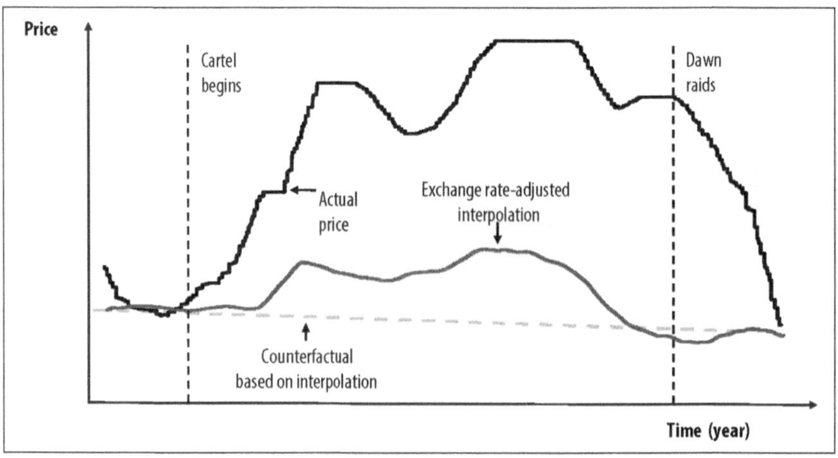

Figure 7: Illustration of price variation resulting from cartel behaviour

Source: Oxera's calculations, based on a real case.

360. A counterfactual based on simple interpolation is rather crude, since it does not take into account any factor that might have influenced the price during the infringement period even in the absence of an infringement. In this example, one of the first things to adjust for is exchange-rate variations. If the price charged depends on values of an exchange rate, it is critical to incorporate this into the relevant benchmark. In the figure above, the exchange rate-adjusted interpolation is shown by the grey line. The difference between the thick black line and the grey line becomes smaller—i.e. the price overcharge imposed by the cartel is not as high as would have been indicated by a simple interpolation.

361. Other factors that might have influenced the price during the infringement are cost-driven factors and demand-driven factors: if the cost of production increased substantially during the infringement period, part of the price variation that might have been considered as a consequence of the cartel behaviour could in fact be explained by genuine competitive factors. Similarly, if demand increases significantly at some point, prices will tend to increase irrespective of whether firms are engaged in a collusive behaviour.

362. Therefore, although simple comparisons can provide some initial pointers as to whether a cartel has affected prices, for a benchmark to be considered robust, it needs to take into account factors that affect price levels in the absence of any collusive behaviour. As explained in Figure 6, before–after analyses can involve the simple comparison of average, some interpolation (or extrapolation), but also some econometric analysis based on time-series for prices, costs and demand factors. In all cases, the aim is to compute the cartel overcharge, which can then be used to compute damage estimates using volumes sold.

4. Difference-in-differences analysis

363. The so-called 'difference-in-differences' analysis is the third type of comparator-based technique listed in Figure 6. It combines the previous two sets of analyses described—an analysis across markets and an analysis over time. For example, such an analysis could entail comparing price variation in France and the UK over time, during the infringement period and after the infringement period. The name difference-in-differences comes from the fact that this analysis takes the price difference between two markets and combines it with the price difference between the infringement period and the non-infringement period. Figure 8 illustrates this approach.

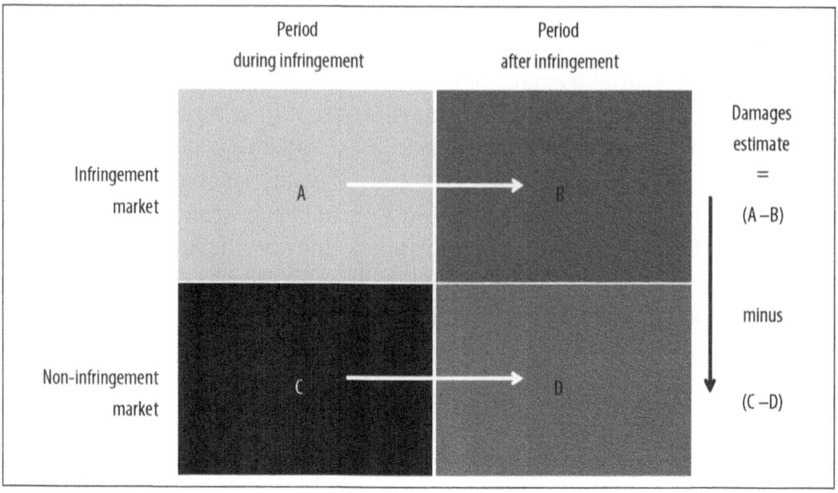

Figure 8: Illustration of the difference-in-differences approach

Source: Oxera.

364. Again, an analysis of this kind could use as few as four figures. For example, consider that a cartel took place in France in 2005–10. Let us assume that the price observed during the infringement period was €12 per unit (A), while the price observed after the infringement was €9 (B). Furthermore, let us assume that during the infringement period, the price in the UK was €11 (C) and after the infringement, €10 (D).

- The cross-sectional analysis discussed above would lead to estimating the overcharge based on the comparison of France with the UK during the infringement, i.e. €12 – €11 = €1 per unit (A – C).
- A before–after type of analysis would compare the price in France during the infringement period (€12) with the price after the infringement (€9), and would find an overcharge of €3 per unit (A – B).
- A difference-in-differences analysis would take both of these elements into account: while the French market experienced a €3 price decrease after the cartel (A – B), the UK market experienced a €1 decrease (€11 – €10, C – D); a €1 decrease in the French price can therefore be justified on the basis of the UK price variation, and the resulting overcharge is estimated at €2 (€3 – €2, or (A – B) – (C – D)).

365. In the same way as the cross-sectional and time-series analyses can develop into much more sophisticated analyses, difference-in-differences analyses are typically used when data is available across different markets or firms over time. The most common form of such analysis is 'panel data' analysis. This involves selecting several firms (or markets), gathering data over time (for example, monthly data over several years) and looking at variation of prices over time when the differences between firms (or markets) have been controlled for using econometric analysis. The advantage of this form of sophisticated analysis is that it provides more precise estimates of the potential harm caused relative to the other two approaches. However, it suffers from the same limitations as the other two methodologies: the benchmark, be it a period or a different market/firm, needs to be sufficiently similar to the period and market where the infringement took place in order to provide a relevant counterfactual, while it also needs to be undeniably competitive.

5. Financial-analysis-based techniques[8]

366. This second category of techniques presented in Figure 6 relies on financial concepts typically associated with corporate finance. The basic concept is to compare the actual performance of the infringing undertaking (or that of the victim) with the performance that could have been expected of the firm in the absence of the practice.

367. One well-known approach is the so-called 'cost-plus' methodology, which consists of calculating the counterfactual price using data on costs plus a 'normal' rate of return. The two elements of this methodology (the 'cost' and the 'plus') can be debated. First, there may be cost allocation issues across business units, for example, or it is also conceivable that, in the context of a cartel, the cartel members' costs were higher than costs that would have been incurred had the practice not taken place.[9] Using actual costs as a proxy for the counterfactual level of costs may therefore be simplistic. However, the focus is more likely to be on estimating the 'plus' element, or the 'normal' rate of return that the company would have earned had the behaviour not taken place.

---

8 Relevant cases for this section: Oberlandesgericht Düsseldorf (OLG) (Düsseldorf higher regional court), VI-2 U (Kart) 8/06 (*Stadtwerke Düsseldorf*), judgment of April 16th 2008. *DSG Retail Ltd & Ors v Revenue & Customs*, United Kingdom First Tier Tribunal (Tax) (2009).

9 Cartel members are less compelled to decrease costs as much as possible due to softer competition in the market. In the presence of a cartel, firms' costs may therefore be higher than the costs that they would have incurred had they competed against one another. This so-called 'X-inefficiency' of firms under limited competitive pressure has been discussed extensively in the economic literature (see, for example, the seminal paper by Leibenstein, Harvey (1966), 'Allocative Efficiency vs. X-Efficiency', *American Economic Review*, 56 (3)).

368. In order to estimate the normal rate of return, several techniques can be used. It is possible to look at similar firms (as in the cross-sectional comparator analysis) or at the performance of the undertaking over time (as in the before–after analysis). In the absence of such information (or as a complement), an alternative approach can entail estimating the cost of capital for the firm in question—the most widely used approach in financial analysis, litigation and regulatory setting is the capital asset pricing model (CAPM). This model is particularly relevant in cases of exclusionary practices: if a competitor ends up being foreclosed from a market as the result of an abuse of a dominant position, the undue profits earned by the company can be calculated using such a methodology.

6. Market-structure-based analysis, using the example of *Cardiff Bus*

369. The third type of methods presented in Figure 6, which can be used to estimate damages in antitrust cases, is market-structure-based. In general, such an approach comprises setting up a theoretical economic model about how the market operates and comparing a collusive outcome with a competitive outcome (or an exclusionary conduct with a competitive outcome). These models are also known as 'simulation models', since they aim to simulate market conditions and outcomes in the presence or absence of collusive or exclusive behaviour. They make theoretical and factual assumptions about how the market operates (which can be criticised) and sometimes require extensive and precise data for calibration (for example, own – and cross-price elasticities).

370. However, such approaches do not always require extensive data. An example where market-structure-based analysis was used and did not require complex data-intensive economic analyses is the *Cardiff Bus* case.[10]

371. In 2008, the UK Office of Fair Trading (OFT) found Cardiff Bus guilty of having abused its dominant position with exclusionary intent on a rival named 2 Travel.[11] When 2 Travel entered the market with its 'no-frills' service, Cardiff Bus had introduced additional (off-peak white ser-

10 Competition Appeal Tribunal, *2 Travel Group Plc (in liquidation) v Cardiff City Transport Services Limited*, 5 July 2012. Oxera published an *Agenda* article on this topic in September 2012 *'What's driving damages? The 2 Travel v Cardiff Bus competition law ruling'*.

11 Office of Fair Trading, 'Abuse of a dominant position by Cardiff Bus', 18 November 2008.

vices) bus routes, which competed directly with 2 Travel's service. 2 Travel subsequently exited after a period of losses.

372. After this finding of an infringement by the OFT, 2 Travel took its case to the Competition Appeal Tribunal (CAT), claiming £50m in damages.[12] The relevant benchmark for the analyses submitted by both parties was the absence of Cardiff Bus's competing service, since that service had been put in place just after 2 Travel had entered and was halted when 2 Travel exited.

373. The key question was therefore how to determine how many Cardiff Bus customers would have used 2 Travel's service and how much profit 2 Travel would have made on each of them. Not all customers using Cardiff Bus's competing service would have used 2 Travel's service, since some of them might also have used other (traditional) Cardiff Bus services. This analysis required a detailed examination of the relative frequency of service, the relative prices, and the types of fare or the allocation of customers across tariff sections. The CAT found that, in the absence of the exclusionary practice, 41,255 additional passengers would have used 2 Travel's service, each bringing an average £0.82, with no additional costs associated with these additional passengers—i.e. it calculated a total of £33,818.79 of lost profits.

374. Eventually, based on detailed analysis of the counterfactual and of 2 Travel's financial management at the time of the infringement, the CAT granted £33,818.79 in lost profits and approximately £60,000 in exemplary damages. The CAT rejected the other five categories of damages suffered argued by 2 Travel. The two main reasons for such low numbers were the precise computation of the lost profits (described above), and the care taken by the court to assess the credibility of 2 Travel's expansion plans—the CAT found that the firm was 'poorly run and administered in almost constant financial difficulty.'[13] The CAT concluded that 2 Travel would have entered insolvency even in the absence of Cardiff Bus's anti-competitive behaviour and therefore refused to award damages on grounds other than lost profits.

---

[12] 2 Travel claimed damages under seven different broad categories: exemplary damages, loss of profits, loss of capital asset, loss of a commercial opportunity (growth of a successful bus company), loss of a commercial opportunity (Swansea depot), wasted staff and management time, costs of liquidation.

[13] Competition Appeal Tribunal (2012), *op. cit.*, para. 54.

Section (III): What about the presumption of harm in cartel cases?[14]

1. What presumption?

375. The Directive states explicitly that in the case of cartel infringements, the courts must presume that the infringement caused harm (Article 16, paragraph 1); although, this presumption can be rebutted by the defendants:

> *1. Member States shall ensure that, in the case of a cartel infringement, it shall be presumed that the infringement caused harm. The infringing undertaking shall have the right to rebut this presumption.*

376. The intent of this presumption is to lighten the burden of proof on cartel victims as well as the cost incurred when suing for damages. In fact, it may be more difficult for claimants to prove harm in the absence of access to the defendants' data and internal documents than for defendants to prove the absence of harm (see recitals 34–35 of the draft Directive). This is not always the case, however, and this difficulty may be overstated: the victim may also be in possession of relevant data, in particular in the context of estimating pass-on.

377. The Commission feels that harm can be presumed on the basis of a finding that more than 9 out of 10 cartels 'indeed cause an illegal overcharge' (section 4.5, page 18 of the explanatory memorandum introducing the draft Directive). This finding is based on a survey of the amount of overcharge calculated for past and discovered cartel cases presented in the Oxera et al. study. The exact figure, referred to in the Practical guide, is that 93% of cartels are found to lead to an overcharge, which justifies the presumption. However, on the basis of the distribution of cartel overcharges listed in that study, the key message is that there is no systematic pattern of overcharge in (discovered) cartel cases. Figure 9 below illustrates that distribution; although, there are 7% of cases where no overcharge was found, the other cases show a wide range of possible overcharge.

378. Moreover, one needs to be careful when interpreting survey results, since they tend to be affected by a publication bias: economists are much

---

[14] On this issue, see also the Oxera Agenda article of July 2013 '*The EU draft Damages Action Directive: another rebuttable presumption to rebut?*'.

more likely to publish an article when an overcharge was found than when there was no overcharge. This means that survey results tend to be biased in favour of cartels with a positive (and possibly large) overcharge, while cartels with no overcharge may be under-represented.

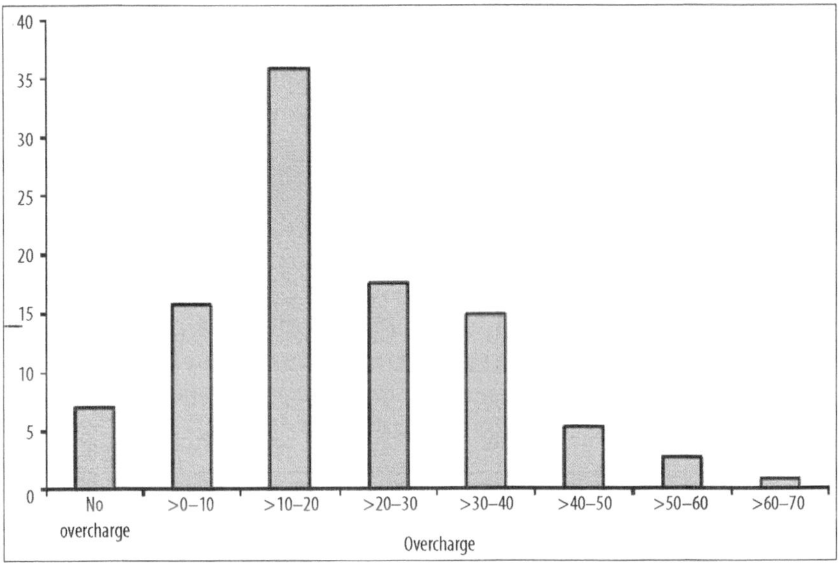

Figure 9: Proportion of (discovered) cartel cases depending on the amount of calculated overcharge (as a proportion of the actual price)

Source: 'Practical guide', paragraph 142.

379. This presumption raises a rather difficult question in terms of the burden of proof: it would be like saying that because a burglar was caught breaking and entering into a house, they must have stolen something. Although this is probably statistically generally the case, no system of law would find it appropriate for the burglar to prove that they did not steal anything. This is what is being asked of the defendant here.

380. Moreover, if harm is presumed, the presumption must be rebuttable using reasonably available information. Albeit this is clearly specified in the Directive ('the infringing undertaking shall have the right to rebut this presumption'), only time will tell whether, in practice, the presumption does not become an automatic starting point, without the effective possibility to convince judges and courts that there may be no overcharge in specific cases (as in the case of infringements by object in front of the European Commission, where it has become virtually impossible to rebut the presumption of anti-competitive effect of infringements by objects).

381. Furthermore, the presumption may sometimes be seen as superfluous, since courts already have the tendency to assume that when a cartel is proven, harm is likely to have been done.[15]

382. Finally, the presumption is explicitly limited to cartels, 'given the secret nature of a cartel, which increases the said information asymmetry and makes it more difficult for the injured party to obtain the necessary evidence to prove the harm' (recital 35 of the draft Directive). Cartels are defined in the draft Directive in the following way (Article 4, paragraph 12):

> *'cartel' means an agreement and/or concerted practice between two or more competitors aimed at coordinating their competitive behaviour on the market and/or influencing the relevant parameters of competition, through practices such as the fixing or coordination of purchase or selling prices or other trading conditions, the allocation of production or sales quotas, the sharing of markets and customers, including bid-rigging, restrictions of imports or exports and/or anti-competitive actions against other competitors.*

383. This definition means that even cases where the practice is an information exchange would be subject to the presumption of harm. Given the European Commission's tendency to rely almost exclusively on an approach of infringement by object, this definition is likely to include cases where the potential economic impact of the practice is not even clear-cut. The potential consequences of a 'hard-core' cartel (for example, where there is evidence of multilateral meetings with price or market shares being set and agreed upon) are not disputed by economists (although actual consequences must be determined on a case-by-case basis, as explained above). The potential consequences of exchanges of information (for example, bilateral discussions around general price trends, without specific prices being agreed) are much less straightforward as a matter of economic theory. Therefore, presuming harm in such cases appears even more excessive than in the case of hard-core cartels.

2. Is there any economic rationale for a presumption of X% overcharge in cartel cases?

384. The Commission's Directive does not go as far as suggesting that the overcharge should be assumed to be X%, leaving open the possibility

[15] See, for example, *LG Dortmund 0 55/02 Kart Vitaminkartell III*, decision 1 April 2004.

for the defendants (or the claimants) to show that it was in fact lower (or higher) than X%.

385. Such a presumption already exists, for example, under Hungarian law. In Hungary, an overcharge of 10% is assumed in cartel cases, for the parties and the judge to rebut. Some economic 'literature' suggests that such a presumption could even be as high as 20%.[16]

386. However, such a presumption would not make much economic sense. As shown above, the results from the survey show a wide range of possible values for the overcharge (including zero). Previous cases offer useful background information, but a case-by-case assessment is still required. It is therefore neither informative nor representative to consider 'typical' values. In addition, observed overcharges are subject to a publication bias: as explained above, typically the most published (or documented) cartels from the past are those that were detected (despite lower public enforcement in the remote past), for which data is available and where the researchers found evidence of an overcharge. This bias could lead to overestimating the amount of overcharge in future cartels, especially if the probability of getting caught increases over time (for example, with widespread leniency programmes or screening systems).

Section (IV): How to go from the benchmark to calculating harm? Applying interest

387. Once the quantum of harm has been estimated (for example, by multiplying the overcharge by the relevant quantities in a cartel case), one last adjustment needs to be made in order to get to the final amount of 'damage' to award a victim—applying interest. This is specifically mentioned in the draft Directive as a necessary step when estimating damage at Article 2.[17]

388. Applying interest, as a matter of economics, makes complete sense. If damage was incurred some time ago, awarding interest is a way of recognising that the amount of money would have earned more money had it been in the hands of the victim the whole time. Instead, it is the infringing undertaking that benefited from having this amount of the money all the

[16] See for example a study by Connor and Lande (2008), 'Cartel overcharges and optimal cartel fines', chapter 88, pp. 2203-18, *in* S.W. Waller (ed), Issues in Competition Law and Policy, volume 3, ABA Section of Antitrust Law.

[17] 'Full compensation [...] shall therefore include [...] payment of interest from the time the harm occurred until the compensation in respect of that harm is paid'.

time between the infringement and the damage award. Interest is therefore typically granted in any damages case in Europe.[18]

389. Nonetheless, even if the principle of applying interest is agreed upon, the level of interest and how to apply it remain open questions, including in the context of the draft Directive. The Commission does not specify the level or the methodology to rely on when applying interest.

390. In some cases, the level of interest awarded by the national courts is based on a statutory rate typically specified by the State every year (for example, in France). This statutory rate can be in line or lower than the risk-free rate for an investment. In such cases, although interest is awarded, it typically does not compensate for the loss in potential interest that the victim could have earned on the amount of damage.

391. In other cases, courts have granted interest based on central bank rates with an additional percentage on top. For example, in the *Cardiff Bus* case, the CAT granted the victim 2% on top of the Bank of England's base rate during the relevant period. In such cases, one wonders whether the court is applying interest on damages, or whether interest is part of the damage itself.

392. Conceptually, an economist could also think that the relevant interest benchmark should be based on the weighted average cost of capital (WACC) in the industry where the victim operates: in the absence of the anti-competitive practice, the WACC of the industry gives an indication of how profitable the amount would have been in the hands of the victim. It is worth noting, however, that this is not the standard approach to applying interest in damages cases, since it requires a careful assessment of the relevant WACC. Nonetheless some ongoing UK cases may well rely much more extensively on this concept in the context of calculating interest on damages.

393. Finally, the way to apply interest may differ between jurisdictions, or even between courts within a jurisdiction: does the court apply simple or compound interest? Simple interest (for example, as used in UK courts since the nineteenth century) means that the amount of interest earned each year is not added to the capital that earns interest the following year. Compound interest, on the other hand, means that interest is earned on

18 It is worth noting that in some countries (for example, in the Middle East), applying interest is not allowed as a consequence of historical traditions and choices, usually linked to religious tenets.

accumulated interest as well as on the initial capital. Compound interest is used in all financial aspects of our life—for example, mortgages, savings accounts, and returns on investment. Applying simple interest is simply never done, since it means that the interest earned each period is not being added to the capital earning interest (which is typically not the case).

394. Table 19 below shows the difference between these two methodologies, assuming an initial capital of €100 and an annual interest rate of 5%. After ten years (not an uncommon time frame for awarding damages), the difference between the two methodologies amounts to €12.9—i.e. 8% of the end-of-period capital value calculated using a compound interest.

Table 19 – Total capital after a number of years using an initial capital of €100 and interest rate of 5% per year, depending on the methodology used

	Initial amount	Year 1	Year 2	Year 3	Year 4	Year 5	Year 10
Simple interest							
Annual interest earned (€)		5	5	5	5	5	5
Capital (€)	100	105	110	115	120	125	150
Compound interest							
Annual interest earned (€)		5.0	5.3	5.5	5.8	6.1	7.8
Capital (€)	100.0	105.0	110.3	115.8	121.6	127.6	162.9
Difference in capital (€)		0.0	0.3	0.8	1.6	2.6	12.9

Source: Author's calculations.

395. This table also highlights how quickly interest can add up to the initial amount of damage. In this case, and even assuming the application of simple interest, after ten years the amount due is 50% more than the amount due at the time of the damage. This is the reason why courts in some countries have traditionally refrained from using high interest rates or from using compound interest rates—i.e. the courts may have felt that it was not 'fair' to award 'inflated' damages simply due to interest rate values or methodology. However, as explained above, in order to fully compensate the victim for the harm done some time in the past, the interest rate used needs to be compounded and to properly reflect the return that the victim could have reasonably expected from owning the money corresponding to the damage when it was incurred.

396. It is therefore clear that, depending on the level of interest rate chosen and the methodology applied (simple vs compound), the final amount of damage awarded can vary greatly, even if the amount of damage at the time of the infringement is the same. The draft Directive imposes only that interest be awarded; it does not specify how its level should be determined or the way it should be implemented. This may ultimately introduce distortions in how antitrust harm is compensated within the EU.

Conclusion

397. The draft Directive sets out a number of principles for ensuring fair compensation of victims of antitrust infringements. The documents published alongside it present, in some detail, the possible methodologies that can be used to properly quantify harm suffered. There is, in fact, a range of methods, from simple to sophisticated, using similar or different data. Simple approaches may be useful in situations where limited data is available (for example, at early stages of an assessment or in jurisdictions where disclosure remains limited), while more complex approaches allow for more certainty around the reliability of the estimates.

398. The draft Directive specifies a presumption of harm in cartel cases, which raises several issues, in terms of burden of proof, as well as in terms of its scope (for example, are cartels really a well-defined category of infringements? Will the presumption be rebuttable in practice?). Furthermore, it is based on a study of past cases, which also raises issues with interpreting this type of evidence in order to put forward such policy choices.

399. Finally, in this paper, we have looked at the issue of awarding interest on damages. Interest is accepted, in principle, in European countries, but the value of the interest rate to use, as well as the way to apply it remain divergent within the EU. The draft Directive does not go beyond stating that interest must be part of the full compensation—i.e. it does not specify ground rules for how it is meant to be applied.

PART II: CRITICAL OBSERVATIONS ON THE PROPOSED PRESUMPTION OF HARM: A DIABOLICAL PRESUMPTION OF PLATONIC HARM...

Thomas Rouhette*

400. The Commission's proposal for a Directive on certain rules governing actions for damages under national law for infringements of the competition law provisions of the Member States and of the European Union, published in June 2013 (the "Proposed Directive"), provides for a rebuttable presumption of harm in cartel infringement cases. Article 16 of the Proposed Directive, which sits in Chapter V ("*Quantification of harm*"), provides that "*Member States shall ensure that, in the case of a cartel infringement, it shall be presumed that the infringement caused harm. The infringing undertaking shall have the right to rebut this presumption*".

401. The defendant to a damages claim will no longer be able to argue on the infringement as the final infringement decision by a competition authority will be binding on the national courts.[1] The defendant will still be theoretically entitled to argue about causation, but this will be somewhat of an uphill battle. As for the third classic element of civil liability, the harm suffered by the injured party, the presumption contained in the Proposed Directive, be it rebuttable, seems to reduce even further the options available to the defendant when it comes to arguing on the principle of liability itself.

402. Such a presumption of harm is rather unusual and original. It departs from fundamental principles of civil liability and procedure. So, one would hope that it is based on rock-solid economic grounds and actually serves a purpose.

* Th. Rouhette, Partner, Hogan Lovells, Paris.

1 Articles 16(1) of Regulation n° 1/2003 and 9 of the Proposed Directive.

403. This article will not focus on the alleged economic rationale behind this suggested presumption. According to the explanatory memorandum published by the Commission,[2] the presumption is "*based on the finding that more than 9 out of 10 cartels indeed cause an illegal overcharge*". The Commission attributes this finding to a detailed study by Oxera, "*Quantifying antitrust damages – Towards non-binding guidance for courts*", released in December 2009.[3] It is, however, relevant to note that the fact that 1 out of 10 cartels does not give rise to an illegal overcharge, for instance because the said cartel was ineffective, is not meaningless. In addition, the author of this study, Oxera itself, in a note published in July 2013 on "*The EU draft Damages Actions Directive: another rebuttable presumption to rebut?*", challenges such a rationale, recalling the limitations of the studies that have been carried out and warning that "*this figure* [9 out of 10] *should be interpreted with care*".[4] Drawing general legal conclusions from debatable empirical statistical data does not look like satisfactory law-making to start with...

404. This article will focus on the legal principles which are distorted by the presumption of harm provided for in the Proposed Directive and on the practical use, if any, of such a presumption for litigants. The following observations do not emanate from a competition law expert, but from a litigator specialised in defending civil liability claims with, therefore, a different approach to the handling of follow-on claims.

Section (I): The distortion of fundamental principles of civil liability and procedure for a debatable purpose

405. Every legal system provides, as a cornerstone, that the plaintiff is imposed the burden of proving the facts he/she alleges (*semper necessitas probandi incumbit ei qui agit).* This principle is particularly well-established in civil liability claims, which are always case-specific.

406. The implementation of a rebuttable presumption of harm in follow-on damages actions therefore breaches such a principle. It leads to a reversal of the burden of proof: the defendant needs to prove that the plaintiff has

2 Section 4.5, p. 18.

3 Accessible at: http://ec.europa.eu/competition/antitrust/actionsdamages/quantification_study.pdf, p. 91.

4 Accessible at: http://www.oxera.com/Latest-Thinking/Agenda/2013/The-EU-draft-Damages-Actions-Directive-another-re.aspx, p. 3.

not suffered harm as a result of the cartel infringement to rebut the presumption. It is a "diabolical presumption" (*probatio diabolica*) whereby, in order to prevail, a party has to prove a negative fact, i.e. the absence of harm suffered by the opposing party.

407. There should accordingly be compelling reasons to reverse the burden of proof. Here, the explanatory memorandum to the Proposed Directive[5] indicates that the presumption of harm aims at alleviating the "*injured party's difficulties and costs*" in proving its case as well as the task of the national courts. Both parties to civil litigation have equal rights and deserve equal attention from the law-makers. The fact that relevant financial or accounting data may be at the disposal of the infringing undertaking is not compelling enough in a context where discovery/disclosure (in common law jurisdictions) and the appointment of Court experts (in civil law jurisdictions) are available. To the contrary, the defendant faces similar if not higher difficulties in bringing the negative proof that the plaintiff has not suffered harm, for instance, when the overcharge has been passed on entirely to the plaintiff's customers, in the circumstances when the passing-on defence is allowed by the Proposed Directive. The infringing undertakings which will be defendants to follow-on actions do generally not have much data, if any, at their disposal to prove such passing-on. Yet, the Proposed Directive does not provide for a "rebuttable presumption" and does not reverse the burden of proving the passing-on. To the contrary, it expressly states that "[t]*he burden of proving that the overcharge was passed on shall rest with the defendant*".[6]

408. It cannot be further alleged that the presumption of harm is justified by the necessity to ensure the protection of the so-called weak party. Experience shows that plaintiffs in follow-on actions are often major corporations, bringing other major corporations to court, not so much SMEs. In addition, third party funding is becoming increasingly available. In the case of individual plaintiffs such as consumers, their claims for damages are likely to be brought through collective redress mechanisms. Consumers will accordingly be supported by an organised group, assisted by sophisticated plaintiffs' counsel and often by consumer associations.[7] They cannot exactly be considered to be a "weak party".

5 *Op. cit.*, n° 1.
6 Proposed Directive, Article 12(1).
7 As an example, Article L. 423-1 of the newly enacted provisions of the French Consumer Code introducing group actions into French law provides that such actions may only be initiated by nationally representative consumer associations.

409. Lastly, the presumption of harm should not be seen as a way to increase the burden on infringing undertakings in a sort of punishment approach. The purpose of civil litigation in Europe is not to punish the wrongdoer but to replace the injured party in the situation it would have found itself had the wrongdoing not occurred. The Commission expressly recognised the specific nature of civil litigation, by looking at ensuring full compensation for the harm suffered[8] and thus rejecting the concept of punitive damages in follow-on actions.

410. One consequently struggles to find compelling policy reasons to justify the presumption of harm and the correlative reversal of the burden of proof.

Section (II): The first of its kind?

411. The concept of presumption of harm is not completely unheard of. There have been exceptions, found by case law, to the classic principle of burden of proof.

412. Presumptions of harm were, for instance, uncovered by the European Court of Human Rights when assessing the harm suffered as a result of breaches of the European Convention on Human Rights. In this very specific area, it has been found that there is a rebuttable presumption of moral harm when judicial proceedings have been excessively lengthy.[9] The European Court of Human Rights has further ruled that "*the acknowledgment of the violation of the right to a reasonable trial triggers a presumption of moral harm thus suffered by the plaintiff and implies a right to compensation without the interested party having to prove the loss suffered*".[10]

413. Similar presumptions of harm have been established in French law,[11] for instance:

- in labour law matters (when the applicable procedure for the dismissal of an employee has not been followed[12] – the dismissal would have occurred anyway had the procedure been strictly followed),

8 Proposed Directive, Article 2(2).
9 ECHR, 29 March 2006, *Apicella c. Italy*, n° 64890/01, § 93.
10 ECHR, 29 July 2008, *Zajac c. Poland*, n° 19817/04, § 84, translated from the French.
11 L. Gratton, *Le Dommage déduit de la faute*, RTD Civ. 2013, p. 275.
12 *Cour de Cassation*, Labour Chamber, 27 June 2001, n° 99-42.216.

- in medical liability matters (when the doctor breached his/her duty to inform the patient about a potential risk which had to be incurred anyway),[13]
- in unfair competition matters (where it has been ruled that "*acts of unfair competition necessarily trigger a commercial disorder that generates harm, be it only moral*").[14]

414. Other examples could also be searched in relation to privacy breaches. In every case where a presumption of harm was uncovered, however, the presumed harm resulted from the violation of a fundamental principle and/or translates into a moral, and not a financial, damage.

415. The presumption of harm in damages actions for infringement of competition law surely involves significant matters of principle. It is however doubtful, at best, that such presumption relates to a moral harm. To the contrary, the explanatory memorandum to the Proposed Directive[15] indicates that the presumption of harm facilitates the quantification of the harm caused by the infringement, in terms of overcharge. The presumption of harm in the Proposed Directive would, therefore, be the first of its kind, as it appears to help plaintiffs seek the reimbursement of the financial harm suffered rather than bring some sort of moral relief.

Section (III): The practical use of the presumption of harm?

416. Plaintiffs who have been injured as a result of infringements in cartel cases seek damages as compensation for the overcharge. The presumption of harm, as described by the Commission, may be considered as a step towards those injured plaintiffs.

417. Yet, what can the practical use of the presumption of harm be? When money, rather than principles, is at stake, as it is very much the case in follow-on actions, how can the existence of a presumption help quantify the said harm? The presumption will be helpful to demonstrate that harm was suffered. But, so what? With or without the presumption, the injured party will still have to provide the supporting elements for the quantification of the harm suffered in order to be allocated meaningful damages.

13 *Cour de Cassation*, 1st Civil Chamber, 3 June 2010, n° 09-13.591.

14 *Cour de Cassation*, Commercial Chamber, 1st July 2003, no. 01-13.052 or 28 September 2010, n° 09-69.272.

15 *Op. cit.*, n° 1.

The Commission's services have also prepared a Practical Guide for quantifying harm in actions for damages based on competition law breaches, which contains detailed developments and methods "*at the disposal of courts and parties*".[16] This seems likely to be more useful to judges and injured parties than a presumption of harm.

418. A comparison with the other areas in which presumptions of harm have been found is telling. In a nutshell, a presumption of harm is only relevant in instances where there is actually... no clear harm or only a symbolic one. In such cases, there is a breach of a rule of principle, albeit formal and without real consequences at the end of the day. The harm derives from the breach and damages are generally allocated to compensate a moral and formal loss (see above).

419. The amounts allocated by the European Court of Human Rights[17] and the French courts in this type of matters are, for instance, often minimal or even symbolic, ranging from one euro to a few thousand euros. It would not make much sense to transpose such an approach to follow-on actions.

420. One can, therefore, wonder whether the distortion of fundamental principles of civil liability and procedure is worth the practical effect or likely lack thereof. The presumption of harm contained in the Proposed Directive would therefore be no more than an innovative idea which could be dropped at no harm to both plaintiffs and defendants, a diabolical presumption of platonic harm.

[16] Commission Staff Working Document, C(2013) 3440, sp. p. 9.

[17] 5,000 PLN, i.e. 1,450 euros, in *re Zajac c. Poland, op. cit.* 10, or 7,700 euros in re *Apicella c. Italy, op. cit.* 9.

PART III: IMPUTABILITY ISSUES IN COLLECTION OF DAMAGES: JOINT LIABILITY, PARENT-SUBSIDIARY RELATIONSHIP, ETC.

Muriel Chagny*, **

421. The title of the topic, which invites to look for imputability issues in the collection of damages, ends quite rightly with "etc." Indeed, imputability is the source of many difficulties in the context of competition law. A leading figure in this field (whose name I will not mention) deems imputability the main issue to solve for judges hearing a case seeking damages.

422. Yet this issue has not been fully solved by the directive proposal,[1] which, as it turns out, does not seem to refer to imputability. This may come as a surprise since competition law, in the area of public enforcement, commonly resorts to imputability on a regular basis in the case of groups of related companies.

423. Nevertheless, imputability itself is also difficult, specifically because of its multiple meanings and uses, "both in and outside of civil liability".[2] Outside of civil liability, it suffices to think of the reasoning adopted, in

---

* The views expressed are personal ones and not those of the CEPC (Commercial Practices Review Commission).

** Academic Director of the Business Law and New Technologies Research Center (DANTE) and of the LLM in Contract and Competition Law (University of Versailles), General Rapporteur of the International League of Competition Law (LIDC) – mc@murielchagny.fr.

1 Even if some changes were made by the Council at its meeting on 2nd Décember 2013 (2013/0185(COD)) and by the European Parliament on 4th February 2014 (COM(2013)0404 C7-0170/2013 – 2013/0185(COD)), the choice has been made to base mainly this written contribution, exactly as the Draft paper and the Speech, on the original "Proposal for a Directive of the European Parliament and of the Council on certain rules governing actions for damages under national law for infringements of the competition law provisions of the Member States and of the European Union", COM(2013) 404, 11 June 2013. These changes will be described in footnotes.

2 P. Jourdain, « Droit à réparation », *J.-Cl. Civ.*, Fasc. 121-10, n° 5; « Recherche sur l'imputabilité en matière de responsabilité civile et pénale », thèse Paris II, 1982; Voy. F. Leduc, « Causalité civile et imputation », *Rev. Lamy dr. civ.* 2007, suppl. n° 40, p. 21.

the context of public enforcement, in relation to the notion of undertaking and parent-subsidiary relationships.

424. As for tort law, imputability can bear, depending on the situation, either a material meaning (in reference to causation or to the link between the factual cause of the injury and the person or the activity of the liable party) or a rather subjective meaning. It is then about measuring the liable party's propensity to sustain a penalty. Furthermore, the problem is compounded by the diversity of solutions in this area among the laws of civil liability of the various Member States.

425. Thus, the choice was made to consider the meaning of imputability in relation to its Latin etymology. Indeed, it is rooted in the Latin word "imputare" meaning "to enter into someone's account."

426. The issues connected to imputability as construed herein are laid down in a slightly disparate chapter of the directive proposal (Chapter III)[3] and, more specifically, in its Articles 9 and 11,[4] respectively, pertaining to the "effect of national decisions" and "joint and several liability."

427. In conjunction with these two provisions, two main questions deserve to capture our attention: To whom can we impute on the basis of public enforcement case law? How to impute between coinfringers in light of the rules of "joint and several liability"?

Section (I): Imputability to the liable part(ies) and binding effect of Competition authorities' decisions

428. Article 9 of the original directive proposal[5] provides that "where national courts rule, in actions for damages under Article 101 or 102 of

---

3 It may be noted in passing that this brief Chapter seems to raise a lot of challenging difficulties. See, as regards limitation periods, P. Akman, "Period of limitations in follow-on competition cases: the elephant in the room?".

4 The effect of consensual settlements on subsequent actions for damages is not dealt with hereafter since a session was dedicated to collective redress and consensual settlements.

5 In comparison, Article 9 of the rewieved Directive proposal (note 2) provides that "1. Member States shall ensure that an infringement of competition law found by a final decision of a national competition authority or a review court is deemed to be irrefutably established for the purposes of an action for damages brought before their national courts under Article 101 or 102 of the Treaty or under national competition law. This provision is without prejudice to the rights and obligations under Article 267 of the Treaty.
2. Member States shall ensure that a final decision referred to in paragraph 1 given in another Member State can be presented before their national courts as evidence in accordance with

the Treaty or under national competition law, on agreements, decisions or practices which are already the subject of a final infringement decision by a national competition authority or by a review court, those courts cannot take decisions running counter to such finding of an infringement."

429. This leads, first, to evaluating this binding effect of competition decisions while considering generally the matter of imputability. Thereafter, attention should be paid to the specific issue of imputability to legal persons of the actions of an undertaking within the meaning of competition law.

1. Imputability on the basis of competition decisions

430. Even though the acknowledgement of a binding effect of national competition authorities' decisions is sometimes debated (as it is in France),[6] this is not the place to revisit the arguments that can be made for or against such a measure. This research paper aims rather at placing emphasis on the scope of this binding effect, both negatively and positively. Not only should imputability be studied in detail in the case where a final decision has found an infringement, but the possibilities of imputability in the presence of other types of competition decisions also warrant attention, albeit more briefly.

1.1. Possible imputability on the basis of decisions other than findings of infringement

431. As soon as the competition authority has rendered a decision other than a finding of infringement, the national courts are not bound. They may adopt a decision in which they impute to the defendant in a civil liability suit anticompetitive practices that infringe Article 101 or 102 TFEU.

432. Among the various possible hypotheses, one in particular draws attention to itself because of its practical importance. It pertains to commitment decisions, adopted under Article 9 of Regulation 1/2003 or

the national legislation, among other, of the fact that an infringement of competition law has occurred."

In any case, the analysis set out in the subsequent paragraphs would not be changed as far as the imputability is concerned.

6 M. Chagny, « La proposition de directive relative aux actions en dommages et intérêts pour pratiques anticoncurrentielles – Changements en vue en droit français de la concurrence, ... de la procédure et de la responsabilité civile », Dalloz 2013, chr. p. 2532.

pursuant to a national rule (for example, Article L. 464-2 of the French Commercial Code).

433. National courts are clearly not bound by such a decision. Yet it raises the question of the evidentiary assistance that victims and national courts may draw from it in order to impute a practice to someone and find him liable.

434. This question is certain to arise in the future, all the more so since the commitment procedure is frequently applied. The risk has seemed serious enough in France to warrant a modification of the legislation; the initial reference to commitments "likely to put an end to the anticompetitive practices" was replaced by "likely to put an end to its competition concerns".[7]

435. Without providing a comprehensive overview of the national statutes, a comparison with Article 9 of Regulation 1/2003 is interesting, this provision stating "Where the Commission intends to adopt a decision requiring that **an infringement be brought to an end** (...)" (emphasis added).

436. We have no knowledge of a judgement that had ruled on this question, outside of a judgement of the French Cour de cassation (Court of Cassation), although it merely ruled on the probative value of a commitment proposal. The commercial division of the Court of Cassation held that the offer to make a commitment before the French Authority does not constitute an admission of liability.[8] This ruling is undoubtedly convincing, but it provides no solution to follow in commitment decisions.

437. In our view, it is possible for a Court to find some probative elements in a commitment decision (competition concerns followed by a voluntary change in behavior or contract can be taken into account as evidence) and, in case of corroborative evidence, to rule that the defendant has committed a civil wrong for which he is liable.

1.2. The differentiated imputability on the basis of an infringement decision

438. Since the proposed provision does not precise the scope of the binding effect as regards defendants, consideration should first be given to

7 "Commitments offered by undertakings and likely to remove competition concerns that may be prohibited practices" in the version amended by the Ordinance of 15 November 2008.

8 Court of Cassation, judgment of 15 November 2011, n° 10-27388.

imputability to the persons involved in the findings of infringement and then to those who are not.

439. *Prima facie*, the imputability to the addressees of an infringement decision should not raise any doubt or difficulty. How can we not admit the imputability to a person, previously found to have committed an infringement, according to a Competition Authority, in view of the Directive Proposal?

440. However, it is not as simple as that, even if the main difficulty, concerning the fact that Competition Law refers to undertakings whereas the Civil Liability Law is based upon legal persons, will be considered later.

441. A first difficulty is presented in the case of vertical restraints when a damages action is brought by an injured party who was, at the same time, liable to restrict or distort competition.

442. Nevertheless, the Court of Justice of the European Union dealt with this difficulty in the Courage Crehan case.[9] A party to a contract liable to restrict or distort competition within the meaning of that provision must not be barred from claiming damages on the sole ground that the claimant is a party to that contract. It is possible to deny a party who is found to bear significant responsibility for the distortion of competition the right to obtain damages from the other contracting party. In that regard, the matters to be taken into account by the competent national court include the economic and legal context in which the parties find themselves and the respective bargaining power and conduct of the two parties to the contract. In particular, it is for the national court to ascertain whether the party who claims to have suffered loss through concluding a contract that is liable to restrict or distort competition found himself in a markedly weaker position than the other party, such as seriously to compromise or even eliminate his freedom to negotiate the terms of the contract and his capacity to avoid the loss or reduce its extent, in particular by availing himself in good time of all the legal remedies available to him.

443. Yet, without refusing a right to compensation to the contracting victim, the latter has nonetheless taken part in the violation of Competition Law, this violation being imputable to him and, thus, he is as much a co-perpetrator as is the party against whom the action has been brought. In the end, it is necessary to think in terms of imputability between coinfringers.[10]

9 CJEU, judgment of 20 September 2001, C-453/99, ECR 2001, I-6297, *Courage*.
10 See II.

444. Moreover, it must be emphasized that the proposed Directive no longer seems to leave room for the "excusable error", contrary to the White Paper: "Once the victim has shown a breach of Article 81 or 82, the infringer should be liable for damages caused unless he demonstrates that the infringement was the result of a genuinely excusable error; an error would be excusable if a reasonable person applying a high standard of care could not have been aware that the conduct restricted competition".[11]

445. As a consequence, the imputability to someone which a national competition authority found to have committed an infringement appears to be automatic, perhaps too automatic?

446. What is to be thought, for example, of the case in which the finding of infringement is linked, not to the contract itself, but to its contribution to the cumulative effect? Thus, it can be highlighted that liability for the cumulative anti-competitive effect can only be attributed to the companies that contribute in a substantial manner to this effect.[12]

447. Also worth noting is the hypothesis recently submitted to the Court of Justice concerning the case in which infringement has resulted from that an undertaking erring as to the lawfulness of its conduct on account of the terms of legal advice given by a lawyer or of the terms of a decision of a national competition authority.[13] Whereas "reliance on wrong legal advice (….) cannot exonerate an undertaking", "errors based on incorrect official statements by competent public entities such as competition authorities and courts" should be "excusable" in some circumstances.[14]

448. How can we deal with the situation in which companies could rely on an exemption regulation that does not apply to them in application of the article 29 of the 1/2003 Regulation?[15] It is indicated in the Guidelines on Vertical Restraints that "a withdrawal decision could only have *ex nunc* effect, which means that the exempted status of the agreements concerned will not be affected until the date at which the withdrawal becomes effective".[16]

---

11 EC, "White Paper on Damages Actions for Breach of the EC Antitrust Rules", COM (2008) 165, 2 April 2008, 6.

12 EC, Guidelines on Vertical Restraints, OJ 2000 C291/1, 19 May 2010, recital 76.

13 CJEU, judgment of 18 June 2013, C-681/11, ECR 2013, I-000, *Schenker*.

14 Commission staff working paper accompanying the White paper on damages actions for breach of the EC antitrust rules {COM(2008) 165 final} SEC(2008) 404, 2 April 2008, recital 179.

15 Council Regulation (EC) No 1/2003 of 16 December 2002 on the implementation of the rules on competition laid down in Articles 81 and 82 of the Treaty, OJ L1, 4 January 2003, p. 1-25

16 See EC, Guidelines on Vertical Restraints (n 12) recital 77.

449. Does this necessarily mean that a Court cannot impute anti-competitive practices to make the contracting parties liable? This is not certain and could lead, in the light of the different examples discussed above, to plead for a return of the excusable error.

450. Turning next to the defendants that were not addressed by the NCA decision itself, there could be difficulties in ascertaining what support this decision provides for damages actions brought against them.

451. The binding effect "should be confined to the scope of the decision", and in particular "to the same individuals, companies or groups of companies which the NCA found" to have infringed competition law.[17]

452. According to Recital 25 of the proposed Directive, the binding effect should apply to the operative part of the decision and its supporting recitals". This appears to be in line with the EU case law according to which the operative part of the decision "must be construed in the light of the reasons upon which it is based".[18]

453. A Court should not impute liability to a person to a defendant that was neither identified in the operative part of the decision nor identified without justification other than the competition decision.[19] For illustrative purposes, relating to a decision by the European Commission, the French Supreme Court overruled a decision for not having specified the participation of all companies whose liability was sought.[20]

454. However, the absence of a finding of infringement for these persons does not shelter them from being held liable.

17 See Commission staff working paper (n 14), recital 154. "The requirement that there is identity of the infringer would ensure that the NCA decision can only be invoked against undertakings that were a party to the NCA proceedings and therefore had the opportunity to make their arguments (…) and to exercise their rights of defence".

18 GCEU, judgement of 8 July 1999, T-266/97, ECR 1999, II-2329, *Vlaamse Televisie Maatsehappij 1/ Commission*, para. 151. See also ECJ, judgment of 16 December 1975, joined cases 40/73 to 48/73, 50/73, 54/73 to 56/73, 111/73, 113/73 and 114/73 – *Suiker Unie and Others v Commission*, ECR 1975, 1663, para 123. Commission staff working paper (n 14), recital 140. "The obligation of national courts not to run counter to a Commission decision concerns the operative part of the decision which must be construed in the light of the statement of the reasons upon which it is based".

19 *Emerson Electric Co c. Morgan Crucible Co PLC*, 2011, CAT 4, B. Rodger, "Why not court? A study of follow-on actions in the UK", Journal of Antitrust Enforcement, Vol. 1, n° 1 (2013), pp. 104-131, p. 116. The action was unsuccessful.

20 See Court of cassation, 15 of November 2011, n° 10-21701, after an infringement decision by the Commission in relation to JCB Services and its subsidiaries.

455. Thus in the same case, the Court of Appeal of Paris, reviewing the case as previously decided by the Court of Cassation, established the participation of a defendant by referring to the recitals of the Commission decision.[21]

456. Similarly, a German Court ruled that "*prima facie* proof could be established for participation in a cartel", although the defendant was not addressed by the FCO's decision itself.[22]

457. The question seems even more interesting in the case of vertical restraints on a large scale. For example, in the French Fragrances case, the French Competition Authority ruled that an anticompetitive agreement existed between the suppliers and a vast majority of the distributors, but without necessarily proving that each distributor had played a part in the infringement.

458. It is also possible to ask how it is conceivable to impute liability to the contracting party of a company previously sentenced for an abuse of dominant position.

459. This question has been raised at least once before a Court. After a NCA infringement decision, sentencing the NMPP for discriminatory unilateral behaviors under Article 102 TFUE, the Commercial Court of Paris issued a decision in an action in damages, not against the NMPP but against its contracting party, RELAIS H. On 27th September 2011, the Court ruled that the perpetrator of the illegal conduct sentenced by the Competition Council and its contracting party were both guilty of anti-competitive behavior. In its ruling, the Court quoted the Competition Council, stating that these unilateral behaviors "were aimed at eliminating the competitors of RELAIS H," and concluded that "it is obvious that unfaithful misconduct was undertaken by NMPP to the sole benefit of RELAIS H", the idea being that a company that benefits from another company's commercial behavior must be considered a co-perpetrator of such behavior. Unfortunately, the case did not go before the Court of Appeals and the ruling thus lends itself to criticism. The violation of Competition Law is only attributable to its perpetrators. Imputability to other persons should not be allowed simply because they benefited from the behavior; other elements are required in order to establish their liability.

---

21 See Court of Appeal of Paris, 26 of June, 2013, RG 12/0441.

22 KG Berlin, judgment of 1 October 2009 (2 U 10/03 Kart) – M. Dietrich and M. Hartmann-Rüppel, "Germany", in I. Knable Gotts (ed.), The Private Competition Enforcement Review, 6th ed., Law Business Research, p. 209.

2. Imputability of an undertaking's actions to legal persons

460. The question of how the actions of an economic unit can be imputed, from the standpoint of civil liability, to the various legal persons combined, according to competition law, into a single undertaking, is, without a doubt, one of the more complex to solve. Thus, one may deplore that the Directive Proposal does not truly deal with this serious difficulty that certain national courts will have to face in cases involving groups of companies.[23]

461. The principles on which competition law rests on this matter are well known. The undertaking is thereby deemed an economic unit even though, from a legal standpoint, it is composed of several natural or legal persons.[24]

462. The erasing of legal persons behind the economic unit, contrary to the independence of legal persons belonging to a group of companies, enables the imputation to the parent company of its subsidiary's actions during the antitrust proceedings. One should then reflect upon the consequences arising from the binding effect acknowledged to infringement decisions on the liability of both the parent company and the subsidiary.

463. Plainly speaking, no specific difficulty arises when both companies have been respectively considered as distinct undertakings, the subsidiary being deemed endowed with actual autonomy from its parent company, since the former is able to define its own commercial strategy and to escape the latter's control.[25] When the competition authority has decided to sanction only one of the legal persons, as it is empowered to do,[26] the situation appears just as straightforward.

464. It is not so, however, when the parent company is jointly liable for the payment of the fine with every other legal person composing the undertaking. On a tort law basis, imputability to the parent company lacks uncontestable grounds. Attention should also be paid to imputability to subsidiaries devoid of autonomy so as to assure that it is still a possibility.

---

23 The question could also be raised, albeit to a lesser extent, in the case of relationships between principals and agents. Connecting the agents to the same economic unit with the principal is justified, in this case, by the circumstance that agents do not bear a significant part of the commercial and financial risks.

24 CJEU, judgment of 3 April 1991, C-41/90, ECR 1991, I-1979, *Höfner*; CJEU, judgment of 18 July 2013, C-501/11 P, ECR 2011, II-0000, *Schindler*, para 102.

25 CJEU, judgment of 14 July 2005 C-65/02 P, ECR 2005, I-6773, *ThyssenKrupp*, para 68.

26 CJEU, judgment of 24 September 2009, C-125/07 P, C-113/07 P, C-135/07 P and C-137/07 P, ECR 2009, I-8681, *Erste Group Bank*, paras 76 to 83.

2.1. Imputability to the parent company in pursuit of a foundation

465. The impossibility of ruling against a final infringement decision rendered in the course, or at the end, of a public enforcement proceeding should result in potential liability of the parent company, to which actions taken by one or more of its subsidiaries are imputed even though the former might not have directly participated in the infringement.

466. Thus, the question is raised of the nature of this civil liability incurred by the parent company: is it personal liability due to a wrongful act, or rather is it vicarious liability?

467. The European courts, before which parent companies have argued that imputation of a fine imposed due to another company's actions constitutes vicarious liability, have refuted this argument; rather, they consider it a case of personal liability and not a no-fault liability (or strict liability),[27] which at times has brought them to draw consequences that were in favor of the parent companies.[28]

468. Yet, from the standpoint of tort law, further analysis is warranted since, according to European case law, "the fact that a parent company and its subsidiary constitute a single undertaking within the meaning of Article 101 TFEU enables the Commission to address a decision imposing fines to the parent company, **without having to establish the personal involvement of the latter in the infringement**" (emphasis added).[29] Actually, the difficulty manifests itself especially where the presumption of imputability due to ownership of the near-totality of the subsidiary's capital is applicable, which in turn implies that imputability is based not on conduct but rather on capital relationships.

469. When imputability rests on the proof that the subsidiary "carries out, in all material respects, the instructions given to it by the parent company",[30] it is easy to connect, from a civil liability point of view, imputability to a

27 CJEU, judgment of 10 September 2009, C-97/08 P, ECR 2009, I-8237, *Akzo Nobel*, para 77. See also Cour of Appeal of Paris, 29 March 2012, RG 2011/01228, traffic signs case

28 CJEU, judgment of 22 January 2013, C-286/11 P, ECR 2013, I-0000, *Tomkins*: the parent company, exclusively sanctioned for its subsidiary's actions, cannot be fined in excess of the latter's penalty; it must furthermore benefit from the reduction of the fine obtained by the subsidiary through an appeal.

29 CJEU, C-97/08 P, *Akzo Nobel*, (n 27) para 59.

30 CJEU, judgment of 14 July 1972, C-48-49 and 51-57/69, ECR 1972, 619, *I.C.I. and Others*, para 133; CJEU, C-97/08 P, *Akzo Nobel*, (n 27).

wrongful conduct attributed to the parent company. It consists in having exerted a decisive influence over its subsidiary's behavior. It is doubtless in such a case that, by not preventing the anticompetitive practice, the parent company contributed personally to the loss sustained by the victim. Hence it can be held liable for it.

470. In such an event, so as to establish whether a subsidiary determines its own behavior on the market, one "is, as a general rule, bound to take into consideration the economic, organizational and legal links which tie that subsidiary to the parent company, which may vary from case to case and cannot therefore be set out in an exhaustive list".[31] "The Commission cannot merely find that the parent company is in a position to exercise decisive influence over the conduct of its subsidiary, but must also check whether that influence was actually exercised".[32]

471. Where the presumption of imputability is applicable, the competition authority need neither show that the parent company was directly and personally involved in the practices, nor that it was aware of the prohibited behavior, nor even that it actually exercised a power of management over the subsidiary during the implementation of these practices. Full ownership of the subsidiary's capital is enough to "presume that the parent company exercises a decisive influence over the commercial policy of the subsidiary".[33]

472. Furthermore, the European Court of Justice has ruled that "the presumption arising from 100% ownership of the capital can apply not only in cases where there is a direct relationship between the parent company and its subsidiary, but also in cases (...) where that relationship is indirect, through an intermediary subsidiary".[34]

473. It then seems hard to link, civilly, the parent company's liability to a personal conduct resulting in the plaintiff's loss and it should rather be seen as a case of vicarious liability based on capital ownership in the subsidiary.

---

31 CJEU, judgment of 19 July 2012, C-628/10 P, ECR 2012, I-0000, *Alliance One International*, para 45; CJEU, judgement of 29 September 2011, C-521/09 P, ECR 2011, I-0000, *Elf Aquitaine*, para 58; CJEU, C-97/08, *Akzo Nobel*, (n 27).

32 GCEU, judgment of 27 October 2010, T-24/05, ECR 2010 II-5329, *Alliance One International Inc. v/ Commission*, para 128.

33 CJEU, C-97/08 P – *Akzo Nobel*, (n 27), para 61; CJEU, judgment of 8 May 2013, C-508/11 P, ECR 2013, nf, *ENI*, para 46 to 52.

34 CJEU, 20 January 2011, C-90/09 P, ECR 2011, I-00001, *General Quimica SA;* see also GCEU, T-24/05, *Alliance One International (n 32)* para. 132.

474. This is all the more true that, even though the presumption is rebuttable by the parent company, who must provide sufficient evidence showing autonomy on the part of the subsidiary, specifically as it relates to the organizational, economic and legal links between its subsidiary and itself,[35] such a presumption is very hard to rebut practically speaking.

475. In particular, the fact that the parent company has not encouraged its subsidiary to commit the infringement or that it was not involved directly in such behavior is irrelevant, these elements being unable to alter the fact that the two entities compose a single economic unit, and as such a single undertaking.[36]

476. Similarly, it is not enough to argue that the subsidiary "had negotiated alone the contracts referred to in the statement of objections, that these contracts were not co-signed by its parent company, that it did not renew its relationship with its distributor and has, ultimately, internalized this function".[37]

477. If the presumption was indeed rebutted in the *Gosselin* case, the circumstances involved were very specific and even exceptional insofar as no meeting of the board or shareholders' general meeting of the subsidiary, where the parent company's representatives were to sit, had taken place before the infringement was committed.[38]

> *"More specifically, to rebut the presumption in question, the parent company would have had to show that the subsidiary could act*

35 CJEU, C-97/08 P, *Akzo Nobel*, (n 27), para 65). See also CJEU, 29 September 2011, *Arkema v/ Commission*, para 41; CJEU, C-90/09 P, *General Quimica SA* (n 34), para 40, 52.

36 See CJEU, C-90/09 P, *General Quimica SA* (n 34), para 102.

37 French Competition Authority, decision n° 12-D-10, 20 March 2012, relating to practices implemented in the animal food sector, para 230.

38 GCEU, judgment of 16 June 2011, T-208/08, ECR 2011, II-3639, *Gosselin v/ Commission*, para 53 *et seq.* Comp. CJEU, judgment of 11 July 2013, C-440/11 P, the Court of Justice sets aside the judgment of the General Court in so far as it annulled the fine imposed on Portielje. The General Court was wrong to hold that the mere fact that Portielje did not take any formal management decision during the period in respect of which it was held to be jointly and severally liable for payment of the fine was sufficient to rebut the presumption of the actual exercise of decisive influence on Gosselin.
See also GCEU, 16 June 2011, T-185/06, ECR 2011, II-2809, *Air Liquide c. Commission*, repealing the Commission's decision as it applies to Air Liquide SA because "*the Commission did not adopt a position on the basis of detailed reasons on the evidence adduced by the applicant in order to rebut the presumption following from its shareholding in Chemoxal and, thus, has not given sufficient reasons for its finding as regards the imputation of the infringement at issue to the applicant.*"

with complete autonomy not only at the operational level but also at the financial level."[39]

478. Yet if the interpretation based on personal liability for a presumed wrongdoing by the parent company fails to fully convince, it remains to this day the only possible one. Despite some doctrinal proposals and national reform drafts, there is no legal provision establishing civil vicarious liability based on control in groups of companies and such a provision is not envisioned by the European drafts on tort law either. Should then the Directive Proposal seize this issue? The question is open and warrants a debate.

2.2. Possible imputability to the subsidiary devoid of autonomy

479. *Prima facie*, the question of whether the subsidiary remains liable for its anticompetitive acts while these have been imputed to the parent company does not seem significant since the victims are free to sue the parent company for damages.

480. This matter is actually far from moot in the case where parent company and subsidiary are located in different States, possibly out of the European Union, or where a corporate restructuring has taken place, for instance disposal of a controlling interest in the subsidiary. If there is no doubt that the former parent company could be found liable under the above conditions, the subsidiary, when it is integrated to a new group, might be tempted to escape any liability by arguing its lack of autonomy. It remains to determine whether such an argument could be accepted.

481. When it comes to fines, the question was asked to the European Commission, which answered it in these terms: "The subsidiary continues to be individually accountable for the anticompetitive practices in which it took part. Any responsibility on the part of the parent company, by reason of the influence and control it exercises over its subsidiary, is additional".[40]

482. Indeed, the matter seems settled, both as it relates to the binding effect of competition decisions and to the right to effectively claim compensation, as well as to the principles of tort law. Even if some national legal

[39] CJEU, C-508/11 P, *ENI* (n 33), para 68.

[40] Commission Decision of 30 November 2005, COMP/38354, Industrial bags, OJ L 282, 26 November 2007, para. 41.

systems, such as French law or Belgian law, have provided for immunity in favor of agents where the principal is responsible for their actions, it is doubtful that a similar solution would be adopted in favor of subsidiaries if parent companies' liability for the group companies is to be recognized.[41] Granting immunity to the subsidiary that perpetrated the damage on the grounds that it merely implemented the parent company's instructions would also go against the effective right to compensation that the victim of an anticompetitive practice enjoys. The fate of the subsidiary should however be examined at the last stage, that of claims for contribution between joint tortfeasors. One could imagine that the eventual contribution from the parent company could be, if not complete, then at least more significant when it has actually dictated its conduct to the subsidiary.

Section (II): Imputability between co-infringers and solidarity rules

483. Article 11 of the Proposed Directive established, on one hand, a shared imputability among co-infringers where the implementation could be difficult, and attaches to it, on the other hand, an exception for the leniency recipient, which is not without raising reservations.

1. The principle: imputability shared among joint and several co-infringers

484. According to article 11§1, "undertakings which have infringed competition law through joint behavior are jointly and severally liable for the damage caused by the infringement." The proposed provision confirms the principle of joint and several liability, seeming to be a common feature of most of Member States. In addition, the subsequent part of the text explains the meaning of this general rule. Nevertheless, the scope of application as well as the consequences call for comments.

41 G. Viney, P. Jourdain et S. Carval, *Les conditions de la responsabilité*, L.G.D.J., 4th ed., 2013, n°s 789-27.

1.1. The scope to be specified of shared imputability

485. With regard to application, we must focus our analysis on the notion of "joint behavior" to which the text refers. Indeed, if Article 11 itself doesn't give any indication, recital 27 indicates that only cases where "several undertakings infringe the competition rules jointly" are concerned, with an addition between parentheses "typically in a case of a cartel" (Pt 4.3.3). This last point solves cartels ruling, but it arouses, conversely, many questions in the other hypotheses.

486. Although vertical restraints are not specifically cited as an example, it is conceivable that there is, as with a horizontal cartel, a shared liability between coinfringers. This is true even though, as it has already been mentioned, one of the parties to the contract would eventually be a victim of the anti-competitive practice in which it took part (for example, because a commitment to purchase exclusively would have forced it to buy at excessive prices).

487. The question is more difficult in the case where it would be characterized, at the same time, as a cartel and an abuse of dominant position. Should we then consider that companies that have participated in the cartel, and those that have committed an abuse of dominant position, have violated competition law by a joint behavior? Similarly, what has to be decided when several companies abuse their collective dominant position?

488. The hypothesis also raises questions already referred to in which, besides the author of the anti-competitive practice, a person is called into question who, with no violation of competition law itself (when only a unilateral practice is being characterized and no collective practice can be established), would nevertheless have acted wrongfully regarding a unilateral practice. In such cases, it is not clear that companies may be deemed to have violated competition law by a joint behavior.

489. Finally, let's imagine that two violations of competition law occur consecutively over time, where authors are partly the same, partly different. Can we or should we apply the joint and several liability rule given by the Proposed Directive? In reality, the issue could be resolved by taking into account the different types of damages for which compensation is sought.

490. Indeed, it is likely that, at least in a French or Belgian approach to the issue, the Proposed Directive should focus much more on the need for a single and indivisible harm. That and the will to insure the victim of an injury imputable to several persons (even if causes are different) should establish the joint and several liability.

491. However, this does not need to take place when each cause generated a different harm. In this case, each person responsible must only respond to the damage being imputable to him. On this point, the statement in the explanatory memorandum, according to which "co-infringers are jointly and severally liable for the entire harm caused by the infringement", is not enough to resolve the problem.

492. An additional difficulty is that the Proposed Directive, based on competition law, still refers to undertakings as economic units and not, as in the civil liability law, to legal persons. As a result, the principle of joint and several liability is intended to apply not only between persons each regarded as undertakings for the purposes of competition law, but also between legal persons constituting a single undertaking under competition law (supra IB). This observation is not without effect when we look at the consequences or the significance of the joint and several liability.

1.2. The complex consequences of shared imputability

493. The main effects of joint and several liability, stated by the directive proposal, are twofold and require a consecutive analysis, first of the relationship between the coinfringers and the victim, and second of the relationship among coinfringers.

494. In the relationship between the coinfringers and the injured party, the focus lies in measuring the extent of the formers' liability towards the latter. "Each of the infringing undertakings is bound to compensate for the harm in full" (Art. 11 § 2). The rule formulated by the Proposed Directive is, at first sight, simple in its principle and protective of the victim's right to compensation. "The injured party may require full compensation from any of (the coinfringers) until he has been fully compensated." It is possible to sue either one single company or several involved companies as joint and several debtors.

495. Yet this rule does raise some difficulties and questions at the implementation stage. We shall first point out that the principle of liability for the entire harm is asserted for each undertaking where the mention of "each person" might be preferable. In the current state of the text, we might wonder whether, according to the rules applicable in the various Member States, the Proposed Directive actually enables joint and several liability of the several legal persons composing, within the meaning of competition law, a single undertaking.

496. Furthermore, and especially with co-infringers located in different Member States, or even out of the European Union, will the most solvent and/or the closest, or even the one connected to the Member State which is the most likely to welcome damages actions, not be the main target of the victims' claims?

497. Nonetheless, difficulties are even greater in the relationship between coinfringers when it comes to shared contribution of the damages. Since the liability is several between them, the Proposed Directive provides in Article 11§3 that "an infringing undertaking may recover a contribution from any other infringing undertaking." A defendant who has compensated the entire harm, has a right to seek contribution from the others.

498. Thus, outside of the exceptions it also mentions,[42] it does not seem to accept other cases where any redress would be closed, notwithstanding, for instance, the fact that a legal person could have followed the instructions of another or even had no other choice than to participate in the competition law infringement.

499. Acknowledgement of a right to redress is most certainly something about which to be pleased, while still keeping in mind that a company held to full compensation of the victim will, for its part, have to split its contribution claim between the different co-infringers, who may be numerous (especially if one considers an agreement between undertakings composed of several legal persons).

500. Let us, however, observe a case in which there will be no claim between coinfringers, but a limitation of the victim's right to compensation. This is a hypothesis in which the coauthor is also the plaintiff suing for damages and will see the extent of his right to indemnification reduced in the proportion that his responsibility bears to the overall harm caused by the coinfringers.

501. Both in this specific case and more generally, the question remains as to how and under what criteria to effectuate final imputability of harm. It is at the contribution stage that the respective share of ultimate liability of each coinfringer has to be determined. The Proposed Directive provides that the amount of the contribution "shall be determined in the light of their relative responsibility" without further information. It is specified under Recital 27 that "the relevant criteria is a matter of applicable national law but pursuant to the principle of effectiveness." The duty will fall upon

42 See above text para 156 et seq.

each national legal system to implement the apportionment of liability in compliance with the principle of effectiveness. One can note, however, that the reference made to "relative responsibility for the harm" might evoke causal intensity or even causal incidence that seem to be the norm under French law, as well as Belgian law, in the event of claims between joint tortfeasors. Yet this criterion leaves the court hearing such a claim with very wide discretion.

502. The Proposed Directive furthermore provides non-exhaustive examples ("etc.") among which one, relating to the role in the cartel, seems connected to the severity of the prohibited conduct, whereas the others (turnover, market share) are rather linked to the incidence of the behavior independent of its seriousness. They, therefore, appear to complement each other.

503. To expand on the same question, even though the respective aims of fines and damages are quite separate (punishment and deterrence on the one hand, indemnification on the other hand), one can ask whether some of the elements that are taken into account in order to assess the amount of fines could not be also taken into account to determine the respective share of each of the coinfringers.

504. Among the relevant facts, we will highlight, on the one hand, personal involvement in the infraction, as a leader or instigator, as well as the measures taken in order to coerce other undertakings into taking part in the infringement and/or any retaliatory measure taken against the other undertakings in order to ensure compliance with the prohibited practice.[43] On the other hand, the fact that the infringement was committed by

---

[43] Guidelines on the method of setting fines imposed pursuant to Article 23(2)(a) of Regulation No 1/2003, OJ C 210, 01 September 2006, p. 2-5, pt. 28: *"The basic amount may be increased where the Commission finds that there are aggravating circumstances, such as: – where an undertaking continues or repeats the same or a similar infringement after the Commission or a national competition authority has made a finding that the undertaking infringed Article 81 or 82: the basic amount will be increased by up to 100% for each such infringement established; refusal to cooperate with or obstruction of the Commission in carrying out its investigations; role of leader in, or instigator of, the infringement; the Commission will also pay particular attention to any steps taken to coerce other undertakings to participate in the infringement and/or any retaliatory measures taken against other undertakings with a view to enforcing the practices constituting the infringement"*. See as ex.: Commission Decision, Gas Insulated Switchgear, COMP/38.899, OJ C 005, 10 January 2008, pp. 7-10, para 514: increase of 50% in the fine for having assumed responsibility for the cartel's secretariat.

negligence,[44] that participation in the infringement was limited, or even a passive role in the prohibited practice,[45] can all be taken into account.

505. When facing a binding competition decision, it is even allowed to wonder whether such circumstances should not be taken into account by the judge called upon to share imputability of the harm between coinfringers. Let us keep in mind in this regard that, pursuant to Recital 25, binding effect "should apply to the operative part of the decision and its supporting recitals."

506. In the event that the competition authority has determined how the final contribution to the fine should be apportioned by setting ratios of responsibility,[46] would such a repartition be applied when the issue is to share civil liability? This question remains open, and warrants a definitive answer, so as to put an end to the too many underlying uncertainties.

2. The exception: Limited imputability in favor of the leniency recipient

507. Paradoxically enough, the Proposed Directive contains a provision lessening the victims' right to compensation by providing for the removal

---

44 CJEU, judgment of 10 December 1985, C-260/82, ECR 1985, 3801, *NSO / Commission*.

45 Guidelines on the method of setting fines (n 43), pt. 29: "The basic amount may be reduced where the Commission finds that mitigating circumstances exist, such as: where the undertaking concerned provides evidence that it terminated the infringement as soon as the Commission intervened: this will not apply to secret agreements or practices (in particular, cartels); where the undertaking provides evidence that the infringement has been committed as a result of negligence; where the undertaking provides evidence that its involvement in the infringement is substantially limited and thus demonstrates that, during the period in which it was party to the offending agreement, it actually avoided applying it by adopting competitive conduct in the market: the mere fact that an undertaking participated in an infringement for a shorter duration than others will not be regarded as a mitigating circumstance since this will already be reflected in the basic amount; where the undertaking concerned has effectively cooperated with the Commission outside the scope of the Leniency Notice and beyond its legal obligation to do so; where the anti-competitive conduct of the undertaking has been authorized or encouraged by public authorities or by legislation". See e.g. CJEU, judgment of 24 March 2011, ERC 2011, II-1223, *Copper and copper alloy fittings sector*.

46 Several coinfringing undertakings can be jointly liable for the payment of the fine (CJEU, judgment of 6 March 1974, C-6/73 & 7/73, ECR 1974, 223, *Commercial solvents*; GCEU, judgment of 3 March 2011, T-117/07 & 121/07, ECR 2011, II-633, *Areva et Alstom v/ Comm*; GCEU, judgment of 3 March 2011, joined cases T-122/07 to 124/07, ERC 2011, II-793, *Siemens*), as long as every one of them participated in the infringement (even in different respects). As to the definitive responsibility for the fine, the General Court considers that the Commission is alone entitled to set ratios of responsibility in the infringement. Joint debtors cannot freely allocate responsibility. In the absence of such an apportionment, the burden should be equally shared.

of joint liability from the immunity recipient and therefore limiting the possibility to impute the harm suffered. This measure of "civil leniency" may be questionable. We can only welcome that the proposal also provides for a return to the general rule of imputability in favor of the victims.

2.1. A questionable measure of civil leniency

508. Without going as far as the Green Paper, which envisioned, among several options, the possibility to grant, as a general rule, "a conditional rebate on damages claim to the successful leniency applicants"; with the clear objective to reward them in the private proceedings,[47] the Proposed Directive reserves civil leniency to the successful immunity applicant, as did the White Paper (Pt 2.9).

509. By exception to the general rule above whereby each of the tortfeasors is, by virtue of joint and several liability, bound to fully compensate the victims suing for damages, the Directive Proposal lightens the obligations imposed on the immunity recipient.

510. As for the scope of liability, it is in principle limited to harm caused to customers or suppliers, whether direct or indirect,[48] imputability of losses sustained by other injured parties being excluded under normal circumstances. In such an event, the claim for contribution is capped at "the amount of the harm it caused to its own direct or indirect purchasers or providers".[49]

511. Moreover, when the restrictive agreement caused harm to other persons than the counterparties of infringing undertakings, the amount of contribution is "determined in the light of its relative responsibility for that

---

47 Green Paper, Damages actions for breach of the EC antitrust rules, COM (2005) 672 final, 20 December 2005, Option 29.

48 Article 11§2 of the Proposal for a Directive (n 2): "Member States shall ensure that an undertaking which has been granted immunity from fines by a competition authority under a leniency programme shall be liable to injured parties other than its direct or indirect purchasers or providers only when such injured parties show that they are unable to obtain full compensation from the other undertakings that were involved in the same infringement of competition law".

49 Article 11§3 of the Proposal for a Directive (n 2): "Member States shall ensure that an infringing undertaking may recover a contribution from any other infringing undertaking, the amount of which shall be determined in the light of their relative responsibility for the harm caused by the infringement. The amount of contribution of an undertaking which has been granted immunity from fines by a competition authority under a leniency programme shall not exceed the amount of the harm it caused to its own direct or indirect purchasers or providers".

harm". This phrase, contained in Article 11§4, does not seem entirely consistent with the explanatory memorandum, according to which "where a cartel has caused harm only to parties other than the customers/providers of the infringing undertakings, the immunity recipient would be responsible only for his share of the harm caused by the cartel" (Pt. 4.3.3).

512. The desired result is clearly stated, namely to safeguard the attractiveness of the leniency programs and in this aim to protect leniency recipients (primary targets of damages actions) from "undue exposure" to damages claims.

513. The stated rationale fails to fully convince because it mentions a desire to "limit the disadvantageous consequences" related to the fact that the leniency recipients to which the decision finding an infringement is "often final for them earlier than for other members of the same cartel" (Pt 4.3.3).

514. One might wonder whether these "disadvantageous consequences" could be significantly lessened if the leniency recipient, "primary target of damages actions" filed by victims, were to bring before the court other parties to the prohibited agreement immediately or at least to pursue contribution proceedings against them.

515. Furthermore, the argument so put forth seems unable to justify the limit on contribution on the part of the immunity recipient, capped at the amount of harm caused to its counterparties, direct or indirect. Moreover, the removal of the joint liability avoids that the immunity recipient has to seek contribution from the other cartelists. In addition, in case of partial insolvency of some infringers, he will not have to bear an increased financial burden. Finally, one may consider that the proposed measure provides for a real civil-side incentive.

516. The proposed Directive limits the victim's choice as to the co-infringers from which he could recover his whole damage. Since the cooperation is already rewarded with immunity, one may have doubts about the appropriateness of such a sacrifice of injured parties' rights given the aim at redress and compensation, rather than punishment that underlies civil liability.[50] It is all the more true that the principle of liability for the entire harm of each tortfeasor is especially justified by the notion of a guarantee for injured parties so as to ensure their complete compensation.

---

50 See M. Chagny, « La prime à la dénonciation (clémence et repentis) », *in La dénonciation en droit privé*, Economica, vol. 32, 2010, p. 137 et seq., esp. n° 20.

2.2. Back to the general rule for the benefit of injured parties

517. As it turns out, by holding that "the protection of immunity recipients cannot interfere with the victims' right to full compensation," the Proposed Directive introduces an exception to the exception and accepts that the relief to the immunity recipient must not be absolute.

518. However, in order to be entitled to sue the immunity recipient, injured parties other than its direct or indirect counterparties must prove that they are unable to recover full compensation from the other undertakings involved in the same infringement to the competition rules.[51]

519. Even though the explanatory memorandum underscores the necessity to "guarantee the effet utile of this exception," engaging Member States to ensure that the victims will still be able to claim compensation for their loss against the leniency recipient, we can only hope that this residual possibility will be an actual one. One may also cast doubt over the necessity to match impunity on a repressive level with limited liability on a civil level.

520. For this reason, the changes suggested in the course of the legislative process by the Council and by the Parliament[52] should be welcomed. It is never too late to do the right thing...

[51] Article 11§2 of the Proposal for a Directive (n 2 and n 49).
[52] Comp. the various versions of article 11 throughout the legislative process.

IV

CONCLUSION

Jacques Bourgeois*

Section (I): Introduction

521. The following comments do not address all provisions of the Directive on certain rules governing actions for damages under national law for infringements of the competition law provisions of the Member States and the European Union (hereafter the Directive).[1] The comments are limited to those provisions that were discussed at the GCLC conference as they appear in the European Commission proposal.[2] Neither do these comments do justice to all papers discussed at the GCLC conference. The book does not do justice either to the spirited exchange of views between judges. Apart from Jacqueline Riffault Silk, they did not submit papers. They were

* Jacques Bourgeois, Consultant, WilmerHale, Brussels. Professor at the College of Europe and Visiting professor at the University of Ghent.

1 At the time of writing, the text on which the Council of the EU and the European Parliament agreed was published i.a. on the website of the European Parliament.

2 COM (2013) 404 final available on the European Commission website.

not invited to do so by the GCLC, which is mindful of the maxim *verba volant, scripta manent.*

Section (II): The aim(s) of the Directive

522. As made clear by its preamble and emphasized by Commissioner Almunia in his keynote speech to the conference the Directive pursues two aims: on the one hand, improving through a set of procedural rules in the EU Member States the effective exercise of the EU right to compensation for damages recognized by the EU Court of Justice as inherent to the direct effect of Articles 101 and 102 TFEU, and on the other hand, to improve the effective application of these provisions as a matter of public policy. After the publication of the Green Paper on antitrust damages (2005) and the White Paper (2008) many doubted that improving damages actions would contribute to a more effective application of the EU competition rules. The argument was that in view of the difficulties of proving infringement of competition rules in court proceedings only "follow-on" damages actions could be brought successfully. Critics concluded that rendering damages actions more claimant-friendly would not create a second way to enforce EU competition rules, alongside the established administration of these rules by the European Commission and national competition authorities.

523. In his report, Barry Rodger puts forward evidence that supports the European Commission's view that damages actions would improve the effective application of EU competition rules. Based on empirical research on comparative private enforcement and collective redress in the EU, Barry Rodger demonstrates that private enforcement through damages actions plays a significant role alongside administrative action. E.g. in the 1999-2012 timeframe out of the total of 213 damages actions 119 were follow-on actions and 94 were standalone actions (Table 8 at paragraph 125 of this volume). Barry Rodger points out that these numbers do not include a "hidden story" of a considerable number of cases settled prior to a court judgment (paragraph 97 of this volume).

Section (III): The effect of national competition authorities decisions on national courts of other Member States

524. Jacqueline Riffault Silk concluded her comprehensive report by stating that extending the binding effect rule would undoubtedly facilitate civil actions for damages. She underlined that the reform as contemplated by the proposed directive implies significant changes in national legislation and should not undermine the necessary protection of the rights of the defense. The intra-EU effect of decisions of national competition authorities was one of the difficult issues in the political discussions in the Council of the EU. There are precedents of administrative decisions of Member States being binding on courts of other Member States. Moreover, some Member States have provisions similar to Article 16 of Regulation 1/2003 with respect to decisions of competition authorities of other Member States. Others do not. Whether the discussions in the Council of the EU reflect a distrust for competition authorities of other Member States or whether Member States were reluctant to have the binding effect of national competition authorities enshrined in an EU rule can be left aside here.

525. A compromise solution was found, Member States must ensure that a final decision of a competition authority of another Member State may, in accordance with the national law, be presented before a national court as at least *prima facie* evidence of infringement of competition law (Article 9 (2) of the Directive). There is some "constructive ambiguity" in the "in accordance with their respective national law". Overall this appears as an acceptable compromise in that defendants may challenge the *prima facie* evidence of infringement of competition law.

Section (IV): On determining liability

526. In the conference mainly two issues linked to determining liability were addressed.

527. The first one concerned the presumption of harm in cartel cases. This was dealt with by Pascale Déchamps in her paper on "Quantification Issues". The Directive states that "Member States shall ensure that it shall be presumed that cartel infringements cause harm. The infringer shall have the right to rebut this presumption" (Article 17 (2)). The preamble justifies this presumption by the need to remedy the information asymmetry and some of the difficulties associated with quantifying antitrust harm. As these factors may play a role in any competition case, limiting the presumption to cartel cases is justified by the secret nature of a cartel, which increases the information asymmetry and makes it more difficult for claimants to obtain the necessary evidence (para. 42). The explanatory memorandum of the proposal of directive refers to a finding based on a survey of past and discovered cartel cases that more than 9 out of 10 cartels cause an illegal overcharge (section 4.5). Pascale Déchamps questions this as she wonders whether, in practice, the presumption does not become an automatic starting point, without the effective possibility to convince judges of the contrary.

528. The second issue of determining liability was dealt in the conference paper of Muriel Chagny. She addressed i.a. the imputability of an infringement of competition rules to the parent company according to the case law of the EU courts for fining purposes. The interpretation based on personal liability for presumed wrongdoing by the parent company fails to fully convince Muriel Chagny. The Directive does not address this issue and leaves unanswered the question whether the liability of the parent company for fining purposes also means civil liability of the parent company for damage caused by the infringement of competition rules.

Section (V): Tort Law Public law in disguise

529. In 1959 Leon Green defended the thesis that the judicial process not infrequently overtops both the immediate facts of a case and legal doctrine, namely interests outside and beyond interests of the immediate party to the litigation.[3] In support of this thesis he found evidence in judicial developments of tort law. The incursions of the EU law in the Member States civil laws on damages are public law in disguise.

530. Before the Directive, there were no EU rules on actions for damages, which remained entirely subject to the laws of EU Member States. In dealing with the relationship between EU competition rules and the rules of Member State law on liability for damages, the Court of Justice of the EU subjects the application of Member State law to the principles of "equivalence" and of "effectiveness".[4] The principle of "effectiveness" has led the Court to give to the enforcement of EU competition rules a qualified or potential precedence over certain rules of Member States laws. In *Courage*[5] this concerned a rule of English law that does not allow a party to an illegal agreement to claim damages from the other party. In *Manfredi* this concerned a rule that limited compensation for actual law (*damnum emergens*) and excluded compensation for loss of profit (*lucrum cessans*).[6]

3 L. Green, "Tort Law Public Law in Disguise" 38 Texas Law Review 2 (1959).

4 i.a. Courage, case 453/99, para. 29; Manfredi, joined cases C-295/04 to C-298/04, para. 62; Kone case C-557/12, para. 24.

5 Courage, para. 29.

6 Manfredi, para. 95; it is unclear whether the applicable Italian rule actually excluded compensation for loss of profit.

Kone involved a rule of Austrian law requiring a claimant to establish an adequate causal link and a link of unlawfulness, which is the infringement of a protective provision, i.e. a "Schutznorm". In the Austrian courts defendants had relied on this rule against a claim for damages based on "umbrella pricing". Referring to the "full effectiveness of Article 101 TFEU" the Court held that the victim of umbrella pricing may obtain compensation for the loss caused by the members of a cartel, even if it did not have contractual links with them, under certain circumstances.[7]

531. In the Directive the EU legislator has effectively endorsed the approach consisting of qualified departures from certain civil principles. Article 3 provides the duty for Member States to comply with the principles of "effectiveness" and "equivalence". The Directive goes even further. It introduces the presumption that cartel infringements cause harm (Art. 17 (2)). The corresponding provision in the Draft Directive was criticized. In his report Thomas Rouhette recognizes that presumption of harm is not completely unheard of and gives a number of examples. However, he rejects that presumption for damages actions for infringements of competition rules, as such actions do not relate to moral harm (paragraphs 411 to 415 of this volume).

532. In her report, Muriel Chagny mentions the example of a French court accepting an action for damages not against the company found by the competition authority to have abused its dominant position, but against the sole beneficiary of the abusive conduct (paragraph 459 of this volume). Muriel Chagny disagrees.

533. Under US law as well there are departures from tort law in damages actions for infringement of competition rules. E.g. in *Hanover Shoe*, the US Supreme Court rejected the passing-on defense on the ground that damages play an important role in the deterrence of cartels.[8]

534. Apart from that, the question arises whether presumption of harm caused by cartels established by the Directive also applies to cartels that do not restrict competition by object. One might suppose that in the eyes of the EU legislator at least some cartels are only prohibited if they restrict competition by effect. So why presume that such cartels cause harm? In her paper Pascale Déchamps voices her doubts as an economist in this regard (paragraph 383 of this volume).

---

7 Kone, para. 33 and 34.

8 392 US 481 (1968).

535. The Directive does not address the question of the imputability of parent company of harm caused by a subsidiary. Would a decision of a competition authority fining a parent company for infringement of competition rules by its subsidiary on the sole ground that the parent company is a 100% shareholder of the subsidiary result in rendering the parent company liable for the harm caused by its subsidiary? Muriel Chagny voices doubts about this as this would not correspond to any of the usual civil law principles (paragraphs 465 to 478 of this volume).

*

* *

536. An EU directive is by definition a *lex imperfecta*. A more complete picture will be available only following the implementation of the Directive in the laws of the EU Member States. Even then the subject matter will hardly be exhaustively dealt with. The papers submitted at the GCLC conference show this.

INDEX

ANNEX

Programme of the 9th Annual Conference on 7 and 8 November 2013

College of Europe
Collège d'Europe

Brugge | Natolin

Global Competition Law Centre

9th ANNUAL CONFERENCE OF THE GCLC

ANTITRUST DAMAGES
IN EU LAW AND POLICY

7-8 NOVEMBER 2013

RESIDENCE PALACE, BRUSSELS

This conference is dedicated to antitrust damages in EU law and policy. It explores the various issues that arise over the life-cycle of an action for damages before national courts, or in the context of alternative dispute resolution proceedings. A key objective of this conference is to discuss the Commission's reform package adopted in June 2013, i.e. the proposed Directive, the non-binding recommendation on collective redress and the Communication on quantifying antitrust harm. Under each of the topics discussed, an academic paper will serve as a platform for discussion.

DAY ONE

8:30 – 9:00 Registration

9:00 – 9:10 Welcome Words

Massimo Merola, Bonelli Erede Pappalardo, President of the GCLC

9:10 – 9:20 Presentation of the Conference

Jacques Derenne, Hogan Lovells and University of Liège (ULg)
Eric Morgan de Rivery, Jones Day

9:20 – 9:50 Keynote Speech by Vice-President Joaquín Almunia

SESSION 1 – STATE OF PLAY OF ANTITRUST DAMAGES IN THE EU AND OVERVIEW OF THE PROPOSED REFORM

Chairman: Jacques Bourgeois, WilmerHale

State of Play of Antitrust Damages in EU and National Law

9.50 – 10:05 **State of Play of Antitrust Damages in EU Law (Case Law and Legislation)**

Caroline Cauffman, University of Maastricht (The Netherlands)

10:05 – 10:20 **State of Play of Antitrust Damages at Member State Level (Case Law and Legislation)**

Barry Rodger, University of Strathclyde, Glasgow (United Kingdom)

10:20 – 11:20 **National Courts' Perspective**

Peter Freeman, Competition Appeal Tribunal (United Kingdom)
Joachim Bornkamm, Bundesgerichtshof, Karlsruhe (Germany)
Jacqueline Riffaut Silk, Cour de cassation (France)

11:20 – 11:35 **Coffee Break**

Overview of the Reform Package

11:35 – 12:05	**Presentation of the Proposal for a Directive, the non-Binding Recommendation and the Communication on Antitrust Harm**
	Eddy de Smijter, European Commission, DG COMP
12:05 – 12:35	**A Policy Perspective on the Reform Package**
	Guido Lobrano, BusinessEurope Augusta Maciulevičiūtė, BEUC
12:35 – 13:05	**Q&A Session**
13-05 – 14:30	**Lunch Break**

SESSION 2 – INITIATING A CLAIM

Chairman: Bernard van de Walle de Ghelcke, Linklaters

Collective redress, Consensual Settlements, and other Incentive Devices

14:30 – 14:45	**Presentation of Research Paper**
	Rafael Amaro, University Paris V (France)
14:45 – 15:45	**Discussion Panel and Q&A Session**
	Assimakis Komninos, White & Case Katrine de Neergaard, Consumer Ombudsman (Denmark) Vincent Smith, British Institute of International & Comparative Law (United Kingdom)

Admissibility Issues: Limitation Periods, Purchaser Standing, Passing On Defenses, etc.

15:50 – 16:05	**Presentation of Research Paper**
	Pinar Akman, School of Law, Leeds University, (United Kingdom)
16:05 – 17:05	**Discussion Panel and Q&A Session**
	Onno Brouwer, Freshfields Raphaël De Coninck, CRA International
17:05 – 17:25	**Coffee Break**

Jurisdictional Issues and Applicable Law: Brussels I, Rome I and II

17:25 – 18:00	**Overview of the Issues and Q&A**
	Patrick Wautelet, University of Liège (ULg) Stephanie Francq, University of Louvain (UCL)
18:00	**Cocktail Drink**

DAY TWO

SESSION 3 – DETERMINING LIABILITY

Chairman: Carles Esteva Mosso, European Commission, DG COMP

Evidentiary Issues: Interplay between Public and Private Enforcement, Access to Documents, Leniency-related Evidence, etc.

08:45 – 09:00 **Presentation of Research Paper**

Sebastian Peyer, University of East Anglia, Centre for Competition Policy (United Kingdom)

09:00 – 10:00 **Discussion Panel and Q&A Session**

Marc van der Woude, General Court of the EU
Eric Barbier de la Serre, Jones Day
Małgorzata Krasnodębska-Tomkiel, Competition Authority (Poland)

10:00 – 10:20 **Coffee Break**

Quantification Issues: Estimating and Calculating Harm, Presumption of Harm in Cartel Cases, etc.

10:20 – 10:35 **Presentation of Research Paper**

Pascale Déchamps, Oxera

10:35 – 11:35 **Discussion Panel and Q&A Session**

Thomas Rouhette, Hogan Lovells
Mario Mariniello, Bruegel
Ioannis Lianos, University College London (United Kingdom)

Imputability Issues in the Collection of Damages: Joint Liability, Parent-Subsidiary Relationships, etc.

11:35 – 11:50 **Presentation of Research Paper**

Muriel Chagny, University of Versailles (France)

11:50 – 12:50 **Discussion Panel and Q&A Session**

Theofanis Christoforou, Legal Service, European Commission
Sir Christopher Bellamy, Linklaters

12.50 – 13:05 **Concluding Remarks**

Nicolas Petit, Director of the GCLC

*

* *

<u>FURTHER INQUIRIES</u>

Charlotte Lousberg
Executive Secretary
Email: info.gclc@coleurope.eu
Website: http://gclc.coleurope.eu

<u>VENUE</u>

Residence Palace
Rue de la Loi 155
B-1040 Brussels

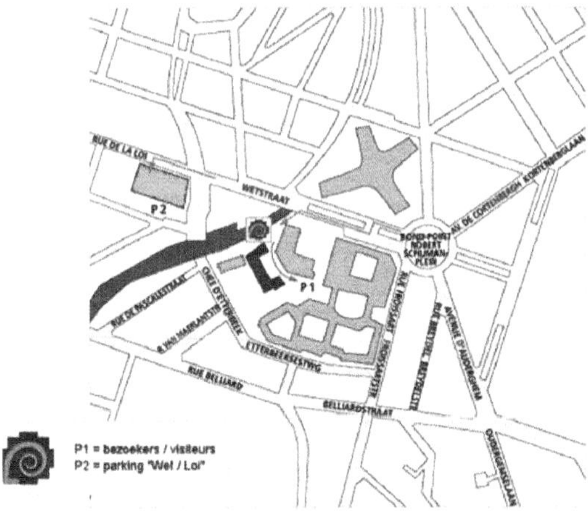